TEENAGERS
Parental Guidance Suggested

Rich Wilkerson

HARVEST HOUSE PUBLISHERS
Eugene, Oregon 97402

ACKNOWLEDGMENTS

My sincere thanks to Helen Hosier, a dear friend and co-laborer, for her countless hours spent with this manuscript. Also to David Wilkerson, Winkie Pratney, Dawson McAllister, and Ralph Torres, whose messages have greatly influenced my desire to help young people. Especially to my cherished parents, John and Bonnie Wilkerson, people of God, whose laboratory was used to develop much of the following material. Most of all to my Lord and Savior, Jesus Christ, for giving me a brand new life.

Except where otherwise indicated, all Scripture quotations in this book are taken from The Holy Bible, New International Version, Copyright © 1978 by the New York International Bible Society. Used by permission of Zondervan Bible Publishers.

TEENAGERS: PARENTAL GUIDANCE SUGGESTED
Formerly HOLD ME WHILE YOU LET ME GO

DEDICATION

To my
beloved and faithful wife
Robyn

FOREWORD

Every parent looks forward to the time when grown children become their friends. It is the culmination of years of investment—energy, time, money, love—all with the goal of raising a responsible, caring adult. Yet, even with this goal clearly in mind, it has become commonplace instead for parents and teens to end up with confused values, compromised standards, severed relationships, and permanently damaged lives. It behooves all parents to examine this critical time of adolescence and discover what is required to successfully make the journey with their teen from childhood to maturity.

The Bible says, ''Train up a child in the way he should go and when he is old he will not depart from it.'' With dynamic impact, Rich Wilkerson has captured for every sincere parent the ''nuts and bolts'' that can make that promise a reality. He understands young people. He has ministered to thousands of hurting youth, and he really knows their heart-cry.

Just as important, he understands how to communicate what he knows in a way that will give serious parents the insight needed to effectively reach out to their teens and aid them as they mature into adulthood. Making the transition from parent to friend is one of life's greatest challenges: Success comes at a high price; failure costs far more.

This is not just another good-advice book, but rather a message which will deepen your understanding of yourself and your child and help you to love more positively. Whether you are a young parent looking forward to the years ahead, a parent in the throes of your teenager's experience, or a parent whose children have long since gone, I heartily recommend this book to you for the future of your family.

—David Wilkerson

CONTENTS

1

Five Things Teens Would Like to Tell Their Parents

Blessed is the man who finds wisdom,
the man who gains understanding.

Proverbs 3:13

Have you ever waited at the airport and watched the partings? Have you noticed how many children are being put on planes alone? More specifically, have you stood in line, waiting to walk on the plane, and observed children clinging to the necks of a mother or father as they exchanged tearful farewells? Have you sat on a plane and heard deep sobs gushing forth from the soul of a child as he or she sits there, all alone, clutching a toy, trying to be brave and hold back the tears?

These are the children of fractured relationships being shipped off to spend time with the mother or the father in some distant city. It's a pathetic sight. The sound of their sobs has stayed with me for days afterward. I find myself wondering what kind of teenagers these children will grow up to be. I know that many of the hurt, confused, and troubled teens I see in school assemblies and in church meetings have come through such heartbreaking experiences. These are young people who are holding a lot of inner pain inside, who have never been able to spill out their gut feelings. These are teenagers who ache to tell their parents some things that are heavy on their hearts—things like the following.

I Have An Adult Body But an Adolescent's Experience

My observations over several years have led me to conclude that a good many parents are expecting too much from their sons and daughters. Many of our teenagers have matured rapidly from the physical standpoint. Some of the fellows have magnificent physiques, well-built torsos, and muscular limbs. They look beyond their years. Many girls are raving beauties when they are only 12 or 13, and by the time they are well along in high school they could easily pass for being 20. They look grownup. But they aren't. Their maturing has been mostly physical.

More than one teenager has confided to me, "I wish my mom and dad didn't expect so much from me." What they are saying is this: I may have an adult body, but I have only an adolescent experience. And that adolescent experience is pretty slight when it comes into confrontation with the heady temptations of the world.

In one of my former places of ministry a 15-year-old girl with middle-class parents and a normal-appearing home situation went on a choir tour with us. She was one of these mature-looking teenagers. Unknown to me, this was the first time she had ever been out of California. When we arrived in Oregon she inquired, "Rich, when can I get my California money changed into Oregon money?"

Now don't misunderstand. She was a sharp gal. Eventually she became an executive secretary. Today she is married and has children of her own. She's a beautiful woman. This incident was a standing joke between us for five years as she was transformed from an unknowing, innocent, mature-looking young girl into a more knowledgeable, poised, and self-assured young lady. At the time this happened she was embarrassed to tears, but it points up how much she had to learn even though she looked like she was a walking encyclopedia.

Girls aren't the only ones who have this problem. I'm reminded of an overnight trip we took with a group of teenagers. We stayed in a large church, with 50 guys in one room on cots and 50 girls in another room bunking the same way. Neither room had windows. When we turned off the lights and closed the doors it was pitch black. I mean it was very dark!

I was standing out in the hall with a couple of other counselors assigned to patrol and keep order. We heard some noise in the fellows' quarters, so I walked in. "Okay, you guys, what's going on in here?"

One 14-year-old kid of fairly average size turned out to be the culprit. He had started a fight. I took him out in the hall and we had a little discussion, with my telling him that we couldn't have that kind of thing going on. I ushered him back into the room where the other fellows were settling in and once more turned off the lights and closed the door.

It didn't take long. More scuffling and noise. I happened to know that he was just a normal kid; he had never been a troublemaker. Once more I went in and told him to head for the hall. "You can't do that," I reminded him. He couldn't offer an explanation, but he apologized, so I let him back in.

When it happened the third time, I knew the boy had a problem. This time he broke down and wept in the hallway. And then I picked up the feeling that the boy was afraid of the dark. I took him away with me into the church foyer where the street lights were streaming in. We sat there together, my arms around his shoulders, with his body convulsing in big sobs.

Here was this muscular kid who had been beating up on the other fellows without provocation, and as I held him up I quietly said, "Hey, buddy, are you afraid of the dark?"

"Yeah," he managed. "I've never been able to sleep with all the lights off."

It was as if he were saying, "I'm an adult boy with an adolescent experience."

We live in a society that thrusts a lot at its kids from an early age on up. They've been hurried through childhood watching violence-saturated television programming and forced to live in stressful situations for which they are emotionally unprepared. *U.S. News & World Report,* in an insightful article entitled "Our Neglected Kids" (August 3, 1982), states: "In a nation that professes to take pride in its young, a maelstrom of social change is inflicting harm—physical and psychological—on millions of children. For them, growing up in America has become an ordeal instead of a joy."

Forced to conform to our rat-race way of living, many of these kids have been deprived of the kind of adult interaction where, in face-to-face discussion with parents, the father and mother come to understand their child's feelings and needs, and are able to help the kid sort out his thoughts. The training they need is so often missing, or at best certain things are demanded with little or no explanation. So they grow into early and late adolescence without the benefit of proper nurturing. They're bewildered, lonely, and sad even though they may act mature on the outside. These are teenagers laughing on the outside and crying on the inside. They may look confident and capable, like they can handle it, and some of them can and do. (And if they can handle it, by all means encourage them to do so.) But deep down they'd like nothing better than for their parents to recognize where they are chronologically, and to help them live through each stage of growing up without expecting more from them than they are emotionally able to handle.

I Don't Want You to Throw Out the Rules

I was very close to a father who had a fine family. It was a closely knit family and his kids obviously loved him. But still, even though they loved him dearly, on the side his kids complained, "Dad is too strict." I heard this off and on for two years from the 18-year-old son, the 16-year-old daughter (who was a cheerleader), and the youngest, a 14-year-old son.

The pretty cheerleader wanted to go to school dances and more parties with her friends. One day I went out to lunch with these teenagers' father and he confided, "Janice is in the forefront at school, you know, and very popular. She's under a lot of pressure to be involved in school functions. Rich, it's tough to be a father. I feel if I let her do some of those things it would be like taking a fine jewel with me into a speedboat and hurling it into the middle of the lake, and then hoping against hope that I'd find it again. My convictions are very strong. I allow my kids to socialize with their friends, but only up to a point. I'm going to stand before God one day and I can't afford to let down one iota on my convictions."

I was able to sympathize with him. I knew what he was going through. But that was five years ago. Today his oldest son is in business with the father. He is married, and they have a darling little girl. The once-popular cheerleader daughter is married, and her husband is the minister of music in a flourishing church. The youngest son graduated from high school with honors and was a star football player. The point is that dad didn't let them down. I remember that on the day we talked together this father cried as he related to me how hard it was to hold the line, and how he knew his teenagers thought he was too strict. I'll never forget his words: "But I do it because I love them too much to throw out the rules."

Parents who compromise with their principles can expect problems. The book of Proverbs is a rich source of practical help for perceptive parents who consistently hold out its truths to their children. We discover that "The Lord's curse is on the house of the wicked, but he blesses the home of the righteous" (Proverbs 3:33).

Children who have been raised according to Biblical precepts are the recipients of a rich heritage. If they hear these proverbs often enough, the words will become fixed in their memory. Consistently the reader is informed not to despise the Lord's discipline nor to resent his rebuke, because the Lord disciplines those he loves, "as a father the son he delights in" (see Proverbs 3:11, 12).

I think it is important for parents to make their children attend church. That is one thing that we as a family did consistently.

After I preached one night, a young woman of about 20 came up to me and remarked, "I'm really against what you said about kids being made to go to church. My mom and dad made us go to church every time the doors were open, and we didn't like it one bit."

I commented to this girl, "Are you serving God today?"

"Oh, yes, I love the Lord with all my heart," was her quick reply.

"What about your older sister? Is she serving God?"

She pointed and answered, "She's sitting right over there with her husband and little boy. They never miss church."

I asked her if she loved her parents. She looked at me as if I were crazy. "Of course we love our parents. They're the finest people in the world. But the way they insisted that we attend church is just one thing we didn't like."

Looking at her intently, I observed, "Well, it looks like it worked."

The point is that when we're young we say we don't like discipline, but deep down inside we're screaming for it. It is the thing that gives us stability. Discipline provides direction and boundaries. It makes it possible for a young person confronted with temptation to say, ''I can't do that because my parents won't allow it,'' or, ''If I do that I'll get in trouble with my folks.'' The blame gets shoved onto the parents; in reality, it is exactly what they want—an out.

When I was a little kid my dad used to snatch me out of the oncoming traffic by my hair. I loved to play in the street, and through my angry tears I would say in effect, ''You don't love me!'' But Dad loved me a whole lot! He was more interested in my having a long life than in my having a terminal romp in the street. Parents need to maintain good rules and enforce them. ''He who spares the rod hates his son, but he who loves him is careful to discipline him'' (Proverbs 13:24). ''Discipline your son, for in that there is hope; do not be a willing party to his death'' (Proverbs 19:18). ''Listen to your father, who gave you life, and do not despise your mother...Get wisdom, discipline and understanding. The father of a righteous man has great joy; he who has a wise son delights in him. May your father and mother be glad; may she who gave you birth rejoice!'' (Proverbs 23:22-25).

Tell Me You Love Me No Matter How I Respond

The third thing teenagers would like to tell their parents is this: ''Throw your arms around me and tell me you love me no matter how I appear to respond. I want you to love me.''

When I was in the eighth grade I lied to my father. I had received two F's in a row in citizenship. I had no problems with my grades otherwise. But every teacher in junior high gave you two grades—one for the subject and one for citizenship. You could have five teachers who loved you to pieces and one who seemed to hate you. None of the kids liked this particular teacher, and they were always doing terrible things to her. A bunch of us dissected a fish in biology and put it in her drawer the day we left for Christmas vacation. No wonder she didn't exactly love me! So she gave me F's two times in a row.

Dad had told me that if I brought home an F that third quarter he would severely punish me. I knew my father wasn't kidding. But even after I tried much harder than usual to keep my mouth shut in class that third quarter, Miss Kleinschmidt still gave me an F in citizenship for the third time in a row.

I was mortified. On the way home that night I changed the grade on my report card with my felt pen from an F to a B (which was quite simple to do). In a moment I felt as if all my worries were over—till I faced my father that night. He was exuberant that I had received a B but deep down inside I was miserable because I knew I had lied to him.

The next day, when I turned my report card back into the homeroom teacher, immediately she could see the big eraser marks, and that the grade had been tampered with. She told me to take a note home to my father to let him know that I had changed the grade! I knew I had had it!

I got home that night and told my parents what I'd done. Dad just said to go into my bedroom and wait for him. As I sat in my bedroom waiting for my father to punish me I felt horrible. Finally Dad walked into the room and sat down in the big green chair across from my bed. I really expected a pretty good licking. But Dad did something far worse than that. He put his head into his hands and began to weep. He wept and wept. He kept saying, "I love you, son, I love you, son, I apologize for not being the father you needed me to be. I apologize for making you think you had to lie to gain my approval." Seeing my big dad weep like that for me was the worst punishment. I loved him so much that it made me feel miserable that I had caused him such pain. When the crying finally stopped (because by now I was weeping as well), Dad told me he wasn't going to spank me that day because he felt like I had already learned my lesson. Then the final part of the punishment came.

Dad made me come over and put my arms around him and kiss him on the lips. I had to do that ever since I was a little boy whenever I got punished. At the end of every punishment Dad hugged me and I had to hug him and tell him I loved him. Then he would tell me how much he loved me, and we would seal it with that kiss. You can imagine a 14-year-old kissing his dad on the lips!

Today my father and I have this very special relationship. When

I come home after being away for several months, I come in and say, "Hi, Mom," and hug and kiss her and then head on up to Dad's office. We'll sit for a couple hours or more before we see anybody else or do anything else. His discipline didn't make me end up hating him; on the contrary, I loved him then and I love him even more now, if that is possible. What I am saying is this: kids want their parents to show love to them even though they say, "Oh, that's too mushy," or act like they don't like it. When I was a teenager my mom would throw her arms around me when I'd burst into the house after school (or after being someplace) and would say, "How you doing, Son?"

Remember, your teenager wants you to tell him you love him, regardless of how he might respond. That kind of loving seals something, and it's a memory that remains.

I Want You to Show and Teach Me About God

My parents always showed me God. They never failed in both showing me and teaching me the attributes of God. In them I saw the love of God. I saw truth, loving-kindness, grace, and mercy. I knew they were always trustworthy.

My wife and I have a young son, Jonfulton. When he was about 16 months old his mother started prayers with him at night. He couldn't talk well, but he did have a stack of Bible story books—little ones with lots of pictures and just a few lines of verse or a very short story. He loved to sit with me and have me read the same story over and over. He never tired of this activity.

But when it came time for bed, Robyn would say, "Okay, Jonfulton, it's time for your prayers; it's time to pray to Jesus." He would walk over to the big rocker in his room. Then one of us would say, "Okay, calm down now, and let's pray." I would lead in prayer, or Robyn would, and he was immediately quiet. Then one of us would say, "Now you pray, Jonfulton," and with his limited vocabulary he would say a few words.

There is an innate desire which begins very early in a child's life for this communion with God. It's not a matter of being raised in a Christian home, but it's just a longing deep within the human heart to know God. God is there, and we know it.

The book of Romans speaks to this restless longing.

> The wrath of God is being revealed from heaven against all the godlessness and wickedness of men who suppress the truth by their wickedness, since what may be known about God is plain to them, because God has made it plain to them. For since the creation of the world God's invisible qualities—his eternal power and divine nature—have been clearly seen, being understood from what has been made, so that men are without excuse (Romans 1:18-20).

This passage tells us clearly that a man's thinking will become futile and his foolish heart will be darkened if he doesn't retain this innate knowledge of God and seek after Him. The responsibility for such early nurturing and consistent instruction as children grow is plainly up to the parents. Teenagers don't want you to quit teaching and showing them about God. They want this developed.

Don't Ever Give Up on Me

The fifth thing teenagers want to tell their parents is this: "I don't ever want you to give up on me."

I recall one mother and father who talked to me on several occasions about their three young sons, ages 20, 18, and 16. This went on over a period of several years, and always there were tears in the eyes of these parents.

These boys finally reached the point where they were dealing in drugs and taking drugs. I knew, as the parents shared these intimate and painful things with me, that if those sons had died right then they would have gone to hell (short of a recent conversion unknown to the parents).

Parents will say to me, "My son is struggling, but really he is a good boy."

They won't admit that their son has some very real and very big problems. They can look at someone else's son and remark, "That kid is going to hell unless he changes his ways," but they won't mouth those words about their own son. But parents, until you admit this, you cannot begin to pray powerfully.

These parents, however, knew and admitted that their sons were in serious trouble. The oldest son, Jerry, was our church printer and had been for three years. He was a good guy and would do anything you asked him to do. He was even fun to be around, although he often came to work stoned. When you work with someone every day, it's sometimes difficult to confront him with his problem. You don't want to rock the boat; you don't want him mad at you.

One day the parents and I had prayer together. The problem had not gone away and the tears still surfaced in their eyes. But the parents were not giving up.

Two weeks later I was walking down the hallway of the church. I passed the print shop, where Jerry was printing with earmuffs on to block out the noise. I waved at him and went on past the door. About ten feet later the Spirit of God stopped me, and in my spirit I heard, "You don't love him." That really brought me to a standstill. I began a conversation with the Lord. "What do You mean, Lord, I don't love Jerry?"

I heard the answer: "That boy has rebelled against his parents and is using drugs. You've known him for three years. You've worked side by side with him, and yet you've never loved him enough to confront him with his sin."

I didn't need anything else. I turned right around and walked back to the print shop door. "Jerry, can I see you in my office for a minute?"

When we reached my office I asked him to sit down. "Jerry, I want to confess to you and apologize to you. The Holy Spirit has convicted me. I haven't really been loving you. I want you to forgive me."

He looked at me with a surprised look. "What do you mean? What are you talking about?"

"You're taking drugs and dealing in drugs; you're rebelling against your parents. You're going against the Word of God, and if you died right now, you'd go to hell. Now correct me if I'm wrong."

Jerry's head hung down. "No, you're right."

"First, I want to ask your forgiveness for not loving you enough to tell you this sooner."

"I forgive you," he said, his voice low.

"Second, I want you to get right with God."

"I'll have to think about that," he responded. We talked for a while and he left my office. But Jerry walked out and called Phil, his brother, and said, "I have to see you tonight after church."

Phil came to church that Wednesday night and Jerry brought him into my office. I said the same thing to him that I had said to his brother Jerry. This young man, now 18, was a big guy. He had been making furniture professionally since he was 14. What I said hit him right between the eyes. In three years I had never seen him weep or break before God, but that night he bowed his head and wept. Between sobs wracking his big frame he managed to say, "I've been coming to this church for 18 years, and this is the first time I ever realized that someone cared enough about me to confront me like this. I'll get right with God. You're exactly right; I have ripped my parents off, and what's worse, I now realize I've been flaunting my fist in God's face." He fell to his knees and got right with God.

The next morning Jerry knocked on my office door. It was 8:30. His face was swollen, his eyes red. At first I thought he had been smoking dope. "What's going on, Jerry?" I questioned.

"I've been up all night," he replied. "My brother Phil prayed for me all night in his room. I heard him. He was crying for me, 'God, save Jerry. God, save him.' I can't live under this kind of pressure. I've got to get things right with God." He did. Right then and there, Jerry got on his knees. Two weeks later their younger brother, Mike, accepted Christ into his life.

All three of these brothers became spiritual dynamos. The church sent them to Bible training school for six weeks in Texas, and when they came back they got involved in our street ministry in Sacramento. They are powerful young men for God today.

One day Jerry came into my office and said he had a letter from Brussels, Belgium. A print shop there, doing printing for the Eastern European countries, had asked him to consider coming over to head up the work. It meant he would have to pay his own way and invest two years of his life in the work. I asked him, "Do you want to go?"

"I'll have to sell my house, my car, and my printing presses here," he said. I looked at this young man, 21 years old at the time, and asked, ''Are you willing?''

''That's no problem,'' he responded without hesitation. Nine months later, on a Sunday evening in our church service, the pastor called Jerry down to the front of the church. His brothers were asked to stand on each side, and his parents stood facing him. We all laid our hands on him and commissioned him into full-time Christian service as we prayed for him.

As I stood at the back of Jerry with my hand on his shoulder, I looked over his shoulder into the faces of his parents. Big tears were streaming down his father's face. I started to weep also. In those few seconds his father and I communicated with our eyes, and he was saying to me, ''Rich, do you remember a few years ago when we came to you? We wept then, too, and our boys were going to hell. We're weeping now, Rich, but these are different kinds of tears. Our boys are all living for God now, and Jerry is even on his way to the mission field.''

Don't ever give up on your teenagers. This is one of the things they would like to tell their parents. There is a promise in the book of Psalms that parents can claim. Read it, and take heart if you are a father or mother who is experiencing that particular pain known so well to parents whose sons and daughters have moved into areas of rebellion that are producing excruciatingly painful results.

> Those who sow in tears
>   will reap with songs of joy.
> He who goes out weeping,
>   carrying seed to sow,
> will return with songs of joy,
>   carrying sheaves with him.
>   —Psalm 126:5,6

2

The Warm Environment

He who fears the Lord has a secure fortress,
and for his children it will be a refuge.

Proverbs 14:26

In speaking to parents across the country I address myself to the subject "What is a teenager looking for in a parent?" The answer to that question seems pretty obvious, but surprisingly, a good many parents honestly don't recognize these basic needs which are so universal.

A Rock

Thomas Jefferson once said, "In matters of taste, float with the waves. In matters of principle, stand like a rock."

Many parents struggle with the difference between tastes and principles; they scream about the way the child walks out of the house and what he or she is wearing. But how many parents are as concerned about what the child is walking out of the house to do? Where is that young, impressionable teenager going? Is he telling you the truth? Do you really know what he is into? Who are his friends?

Parents often do not distinguish between personal tastes and Biblical principles. They are so caught up in what their friends will think and say, and in making the right impression, that they major on the minors. Parents are yelling about trivial matters but not teaching Biblical truth. Jesus had something to say about the structure of the building and emphasized the necessity for a firm foundation for the living church. Of course He wasn't referring to a mere building made with wood, nails, bricks, and mortar when He said, "...you are Peter, and on this rock I will build my church, and the gates of hell will not overcome it" (Matthew 16:18).

The Church is comprised of people, and if the Word of the living Lord is to be preserved from generation to generation, it will take parents standing on Biblical principles and imparting those life-changing truths to their children—to other Peters. The name *Peter* meant *stone*. Jesus was saying, "You are Peter, a stone," but then, referring to Himself, He said, "...on *this* rock I will build my church, and all the powers of hell shall not prevail against it."

Elsewhere in the Bible we see passages which speak of Christ as the only Foundation of the living church. (See 1 Corinthians 3:11, 1 Peter 2:6-8.) How important that we impart these fundamental truths to our teenagers—that Christ is both the Founder and the Foundation of the church, and if there is to be any stability in our lives, it will come only as we are built on and built up in Him.

Certainly in our society the forces of hell have come against the church and the family structure. The family as a unit, comprising the church as a body, has been attacked as never before. In today's increasingly rootless society, powerful forces and influences have been tearing away at the fabric of the traditional American family. One writer described where the American family is headed in an article entitled "Family Life by the Year 2000": "It seems probable that the important education of the infant and toddler will not be left to the haphazard and amateurish efforts of parents but will be carried out by experts....There will be *some* room for individuality, but I predict experts will be teaching most infants."[1]

Perhaps you think that sounds farfetched and even ridiculous. (I shall have more to say on this subject in the next chapter.) *U.S. News & World Report* (August 9, 1982) informs us that the U.S. Department of Health and Human Services estimates that there are 20,000 day-care centers in this country that are open at least ten hours a day. It also notes that there are some 100,000 family day-care homes, with only about 5 percent of them licensed. Overall, according to federal estimates, eight to ten million youngsters of ages six and under are in a child-care situation. In addition to this, before-and-after school programs exist in about 100 public-school districts. (This doesn't even take into account the many private and Christian schools which offer this same type of program.)

The tragedy is that these are not all staffed by "experts," and even if they were, what they might consider to be "expert" care in many instances could not qualify for the kind of training and "rootedness" in godly principles that Jesus Himself was referring to. Many of these centers are staffed by poorly paid and underqualified individuals. The ingredient most needed—love and tender nurturing care—is sometimes missing. Many of today's teenagers have come up through such kinds of institutionalized child-care centers; they haven't experienced that true shelter in the time of their personal storms that they so desperately needed. That rocklike influence providing stability and security has been missing. What these teenagers are crying out for—if not audibly, then certainly in their actions—is a rocklike parental influence upon which they can safely lean—mothers and fathers who will not crumble when the storms assail because they themselves are rooted and grounded upon the Rock, Christ Jesus.

One of the problems I see parents struggling with is compromising of principles. Of course these kids are going to test their parents. It's a very common thing. "Aw, come one, Mom, come on, Dad, everybody else gets to do it." Why do parents cave in? They compromise principles in order to please their children. But it usually doesn't work. Parents decide to let down in one area but their children still aren't satisfied. So they agree to compromise in another area—anything to keep the peace, you know.

Compromising of principles often comes about because it's just plain tough work to keep up high standards. Tired parents capitulate. Too often, working dads and moms simply don't have the stamina to stand up to the pressure of their teenagers' persistent demands. Some parents have three (sometimes more) teenagers to handle. Or there may be one teenager and two or three little children, all with demands that must be met. Life pulls us in many directions.

Other parents compromise principles because they haven't really decided for themselves what they believe, and they haven't agreed, as husbands and wives, what their united goals should be for their family. There are gray areas in certain matters; they aren't truly one. Teenagers are quick to use this to their own advantage as they pit one parent against the other.

There is a solid Biblical principle upon which parents should be building together, and it relates to providing for the needs of one's immediate family (see 1 Timothy 5:8). When I've pointed this out to husbands and wives they are quick to jump to their own defense. "What do you mean? I provide for my family's needs. I provide well for them. Ask my wife. I bring home a good paycheck, don't I, honey?"

There are some provisions in life which can't be bought with a good paycheck. These are the intangibles, like giving of one's self and one's undivided attention to that teenager craving to have an audience with you, his busy parent. It's your refusal to compromise principles just to keep the peace that your teenager wants and needs. It's a firmness that may appear to be uncompromising and tough but in reality is tender and strong. Upon serious reflection, and upon viewing the problems and heartaches that their friends have brought upon themselves as their parents have caved in, your teenager will finally recognize that what you said and did was in his or her best interests.

Jesus said it, and it can't be improved upon: "What good is it for a man to gain the whole world, yet forfeit his soul?" (Mark 8:36). That's too high a price to pay when you translate that to say, "What good is it for a parent to gain prestige, temporary peace with his teenagers, and popularity among his teenagers' friends, yet forfeit his children's souls?"

Everything around us today is changing. We are living in a world of instant everything. Little time is being invested in that which is stable and enduring—like a happy family. Somewhere in their lives these teenagers need a rock—someone who isn't changing, someone who is immovable. That someone should be *you*, their mother and their father.

Someone Who Is Not Like Them

I firmly believe that young people need someone who is *not* like them. It's important that *you* be adult and parental. Many parents think that they have to get down on their teenager's level and talk and look "cool." All day long your teenager struggles with other young people who are trying to impress one another. They get ripped off much of the time. When they come home they don't want to try to keep up with a cool parent. *They want you to be a parent.*

They don't expect their fathers to be "Mr. Cool." They don't want you to compete with them. Home is to be a haven—a place of refuge, a resting place, a place where they can truly relax and feel secure. So when your child calls you "square" or complains that you're "not with it" or "someone from another planet," don't worry. *You* are the parents, remember!

One woman, reminiscing about her parents and the childhood she enjoyed, spoke of them as being noticeably different in contrast to her friends' parents. "They loved us with special sweetness." These wise parents didn't try to fit in with the current fads of their daughter's era, but they held the line, as it were, maintaining open communication while upholding a Biblical standard.

Someone to Encourage Them

I believe that young people are looking for someone who will encourage them. Elsewhere I discuss the low self-esteem which so many young people in this nation have today. They don't feel good enough. People at school cut them down, and in their after-school jobs they get the same treatment. Adults have a way of demeaning teenagers that comes like a slap in the face. What looks like cockiness is a bravado as false as a counterfeit ten-dollar bill. This pretense posing as deviant confidence masks the hurt and loneliness that these teenagers are feeling.

All day long it's a rat race for them. Adults think they have it rough and that life is one long, tedious rat race—and for many adults it is—but it's not easy to be a teenager either in today's complicated society. Though their material needs are often being met very well, many children today aren't seeing their parents enough, and when they do see them, the parents boast about making it "quality time" even if it isn't "quantity time."

In reality it frequently isn't either one of these. The kids know it best because they are the ones who need the encouragement. The frantic pace that parents are keeping often leaves little time for pats on the back, warm hugs, and all the little things that still mean a lot to teenagers. When kids come home from school they need an encourager. Lacking this, a child often feels uncared-for. David Elkind, psychologist and author of *The Hurried Child: Growing Up Too Fast Too Soon,* when asked about the impact of emotional strains on children, commented: "We see many more children who show symptoms of stress—headaches, stomachaches, low mood, learning problems. As they get older, many feel that they have missed an important part of their life. They feel used and abused.

"My concern is that if they don't feel cared about, then they can't ever care about anybody else—or about themselves. We may be creating a large number of children who are emotional misfits. We already see it in colleges, where many young people are much less resilient than before."[2]

What is the result of this? What happens when children and teenagers don't receive love and encouragement? More and more children and teenagers today are becoming maladjusted. Dr. Elkind has this analysis: "There's a delayed effect. From age 6 to 12, children tend to be very adult-oriented; they want to please. Suddenly, adolescence comes along, and these kids begin to rehash the things that happened when they were children—being used as confidants, being pushed to care for themselves and to achieve.

"Parents are often amazed at how angry these teenagers are because it seems out of proportion to immediate events. When they rebel, teenagers often use adult ways of reducing stress—drugs, alcohol, sexual promiscuity. Suicides also are up substantially."[3]

Parents need to ask themselves some questions: What things am I encouraging in my children? A naughty child who gets lots of attention soon catches on and, in effect, is being *encouraged* to misbehave. Children learn early in life that when they complain about not feeling well they get attention. To what extent do we *encourage* our children and teenagers in these negative ways? In contrast, how much encouragement and commendation do we give the child or teenager who excels and/or does a good job in some work effort?

A friend of mine remarks that a pat on the back is a lot more encouragement than a kick in the pants. Somehow I get the feeling that this person received more of the former than she did encouragement in her pursuits. By failing to encourage our teenagers we are discouraging them. Does God, as our heavenly Father, deal with us this way? Aren't He and His Son to be our example? God looks past our failures and assures us in His Word that He understands the reasons for our distress. We often have to suffer the consequences for our behavior, but He still meets us with pardon, grace, mercy, love, acceptance, and correction—and along with this there is encouragement. Someone has pointed out that God is both supportive and consistent. Out of His loving and just nature God has established controls that provide the right balance between freedom and restraint. As Don Highlander emphasizes in *Positive Parenting*, "God is accessible, approachable, and reachable. He responds to our need for love and guidance and is both firm and kind in the way that he communicates with us.

"When we begin to understand how God deals with us in tender, loving encouragement, we understand our value to him. And we see the *model* of the kind of relationship we are to have with our children."[4]

Our teenagers need to be shown that, not only is encouragement from others desirable, and they themselves are to cultivate this Christian grace and extend it to others, but they don't have to depend on such encouragement from outside sources. We can point out to them, for example, the story of David. At one point in his experience David's two wives had been captured by his enemies, and he and his men found that their sons and daughters, as well as their wives, had been taken captive. David was greatly distressed because even his own men were talking of stoning him, and each one was bitter in his spirit because of these circumstances. What would our young people do today if they were confronted with similar tragic circumstances? The Bible supplies the answer as to what David did. We read that "David encouraged himself in the Lord his God" (1 Samuel 30:6 KJV).

We have an example in the Bible of what encouragement can mean to someone. In Acts 13 we see Paul and Barnabas setting off on their first missionary journey. With them was young John Mark. But en route, in Pamphylia, the boy must have become discouraged. At any rate, he left them and returned home.

In Acts 15 Paul and Barnabas are getting ready to set out on another missionary journey. Barnabas wanted to take John Mark along again, "but Paul did not think it wise to take him, because he had deserted them in Pamphylia and had not continued with them in the work. They had such a sharp disagreement that they parted company. Barnabas took Mark and sailed for Cyprus, but Paul chose Silas and left, commended by the brothers to the grace of the Lord" (verses 38-40).

Later, in 2 Timothy 4:11, apparently under Barnabas's watchful eye and encouragement, John Mark proved himself worthy of Barnabas's concern and care, because now Paul is writing a letter and making some requests. One of those requests states: "Get Mark and bring him with you, because he is helpful to me in my ministry."

How did that young boy become profitable? Because of his Uncle Barnabas. The name "Barnabas" means "son of encouragement." Barnabas was the father figure in John Mark's life who stood by and stroked him and said, "You'll be okay. You can make it. Sure you blew it the first time, but we all make mistakes. I've got confidence in you."

How long has it been since you encouraged your teenager? Do you remember a time in your life when you were really down? Maybe it was when you were little and you crawled up on your dad's knee or hung on your mother's skirt and she reached down and gave you a big hug. Maybe it was a phone call when you said, "I've got a problem..." and your parents encouraged you. You hung up and you believed it. That's what *your* teenager needs from you today.

Someone with Compassion

Teenagers need lots of love. I'm referring to agape-type love. That's love with commitment. That's love that is not just based on feeling. It's a choice you make to be committed no matter what the other person does in return.

This kind of love calls for acceptance. A mother came up to me in the southwest part of the country and said, "Mr. Wilkerson, I just don't believe I can handle it anymore."

I looked at that distraught mother and said, "It's called 1 Corinthians 10:13 love: 'No temptation has seized you except what is common to man. And God is faithful; he will not let you be tempted beyond what you can bear. But when you are tempted, he will also provide a way out so that you can stand up under it.' You aren't alone in your temptation to throw in the towel. But you can handle it—yes, you can.''

Parents come up and wail, "I'm going to give up."

I respond, "No, there's a lot more strength in you that you don't even know about. You go back home and tap into it. Tap into Him. Yes, you can show the compassion and acceptance your son or daughter needs. *That's why you're the parent.*"

Parents walk away believing it.

Acceptance. Compassion. You don't have to accept your child's sin, *but you accept him as a person.* He is your child. You can say, "I accept you. You always have a place in our hearts and in our home. We love you."

I'm not talking about compromising your principles. I'm talking about another dimension in this thing called compassion. It's called forgiveness. Jesus once said that we are to forgive seventy times seven. He meant, of course, that we don't keep a record. Perhaps it will total out to be once every two minutes, or at least it may seem that often! If you are forgiving your children that often it's going to be pretty difficult to find cause to criticize them!

Someone with the Ability to Cope

A teenager is looking for someone with the ability to cope. Some of his friends are coping by copping out on drugs or alcohol; others are openly rebelling or engaging in sexual misconduct. Someone must show him how to cope with the frustrations and disappointments that life throws his way. Will your teenager be a statistic—one out of nine who can be expected to appear in juvenile court before he turns 18? Will he be one of the grim number among the million who run away from home each year, some never to return? Will your daughter turn to sex to fulfill the needs in her life—one out of ten who becomes a teenage mother or resorts to abortion? Will your teenager be part of the answer or part of the problem? What have they learned from you about coping?

How Do You Handle Success?

Can you handle success, or does it go to your head? Do you know what to do with the power that often accompanies success? Do you step on the little guy to get toward the top? Because of your success do you give the impression that you're the most powerful parent on the block?

Joshua 1 tells us how to have good success. How do you measure up to these instructions? "Be strong and very courageous. Be careful to obey all the law my servant Moses gave you; do not turn from it to the right or to the left, that you may be successful wherever you go. Do not let this Book of the Law depart from your mouth; meditate on it day and night, so that you may be careful to do everything written in it. Then you will be prosperous and successful" (verses 7 and 8).

How Do You Cope with Anger?

Do you blow up at the drop of a hat? I have visited families where the noise level was always high—that's the way they talked to each other about everything. "GO TO THE BATHROOM!" So the kid responds, "OKAY!"

What has happened over the years is that mom and dad have spoken louder and louder until normal to them is shouting. You can imagine the kinds of explosions that occur in that kind of setting just to get someone's attention.

How do you handle anger? Proverbs 19:11 tells us how to cope with irritations that can lead to explosions: "A man's wisdom gives him patience; it is to his glory to overlook an offense." You've got to admit that this is pretty potent advice!

Colossians 3:8 instructs, "But now you must rid yourselves of all such things as these: anger, rage, malice, slander, and filthy language from your lips."

The way you handle anger is the way your child will learn to deal with it.

How Do You Cope with Failure?

David sustained his faith by the power of God. In Psalm 27 he spells out the many things that conspired to strike fear and terror in his heart. Trouble was no foreigner to him. David had plenty of enemies. Tears and crying out to the Lord were almost a daily experience, especially at certain times in his life. False witnesses rose up against him. He really felt like a failure on many occasions. After rehearsing all these things, he adds, "I had fainted unless I had believed to see the goodness of the Lord in the land of the living. Wait on the Lord; be of good courage, and he shall strengthen thine heart; wait, I say, on the Lord" (verses 13 and 14 KJV).

Does the responsibility of being the parent of a teenager nearly drive you up the wall? Have some of the problems almost buried you? Do you bring up the dismal past so often that your teenager can't talk or act positively no matter how hard he tries? What are you projecting to your teenager by the way you handle failure? If this is a major problem with you, I would like to suggest that you waste no time in obtaining the book *Failure: The Back Door To Success,* by Erwin W. Lutzer. We are an overanalyzed, undermotivated, guilt-ridden society. We haven't learned what God's standard of success is, nor what failure actually is. Neither have we learned to apply God's remedy for this or *all* problems. What we need is a true perspective; what our teenagers need is to see us handling failure in a victorious way despite what may well be incredibly bad circumstances. Yes, there will be times when we feel we've failed God and those we love the most. But by God's grace we can show our teenagers that God specializes in success and in doing the impossible. We have a big God who can perform big miracles.

Everyone—including some of the greatest saints who have ever lived—has experienced regret, some unbelief at times, and the reality of failure. There are literally thousands of verses in the Bible that can be applied to whatever it is that is causing you to struggle. I could give them to you, but I think you need to search them out for yourself. In the very searching your teenager may see you coping with failure in a way that will be a positive encouragement to him and an example that will last him a lifetime. Here are some strong words to nudge you into thinking: "Humble yourselves, therefore, under God's mighty hand, that he may lift you up in due time. Cast all your anxiety on him because he cares for you. Be self-controlled and alert. Your enemy the devil prowls around like a roaring lion looking for someone to devour. Resist him, standing firm in the faith" (1 Peter 5:6-9a).

NOTES

1. Marjorie East, "Family Life by the Year 2000," in *Journal of Home Economics,* vol. 62, no. 1, Jan. 1970, p. 15.
2. *U.S. News & World Report,* Aug. 9, 1982, p. 58.
3. Ibid.
4. Don Highlander, *Positive Parenting* (Waco, Texas: Word Books, 1980).

3

Being What Your Teenager Needs

By wisdom a house is built,
and through understanding it is established;
through knowledge its rooms are filled
with rare and beautiful treasures.

Proverbs 24:3,4

It's not just Christian books, religious periodicals, and radio and television programs with a distinctly Christian slant that are sounding the warning, but secular writers in books and magazine articles, plus radio and television programs that make no claim whatever to anything religious, are picking up the refrain. That warning was worded like this in *U.S. News & World Report* (August 9, 1982): "Our Neglected Kids—Most of them are properly clothed and fed, but something is missing in the lives of countless children. For many, it is a matter of needing more attention from parents caught up in everyday pressures."

Did you catch that phrase *"a matter of needing more attention from parents"*? In one way or another, that's the message being beamed to the American public with increasing regularity. John Merrow, executive producer of the Public Broadcasting Service's series "Your Children, My Children," has stated that "there is an antichild spirit loose in the land."[1]

Alvin Toffler challenged the thinking of the American people with his controversial 1970 best-seller, *Future Shock*. More recently, in his 1980 book, *The Third Wave,* Toffler has identified yet another revolutionary phenomenon sweeping across the land—the crack-up of all institutions spawned by the Second Wave, the industrial revolution, but primarily the fracture of the family. The traumatic process is altering the family system almost beyond recognition.

The First Wave of change in this nation was caused by the development of agriculture, according to Toffler, and the Second Wave was the industrial revolution, but this Third Wave is creating a new family system supplanting the one that characterized the Second Wave. Toffler sees both pluses and minuses in this new Third Wave civilization, but warns of the agonies of transition that must be dealt with. There will be increasing diversity that, for many people, will prove to be more bewildering than helpful.

We are one of the technologically advanced nations honeycombed with a bewildering array of family forms. To name some of these: homosexual marriages, communes, elderly people banding together, tribal groupings among certain minorities, contract marriages, family clusters, and a variety of intimate networks with or without shared sex, as well as families in which mother and father live and work in different cities. All this points to the breakdown of the nuclear family— i.e., a husband-breadwinner, a wife-housekeeper, and a number of children. There has been a spectacular increase in the number of single-parent families. A little-recognized but accurate figure reveals that a staggering 20 percent of American children live in a one-parent family. Then there are those families which Toffler terms the "aggregate family," in which two divorced couples with children remarry, bringing the children of both marriages into a new, expanded family form. Already 25 percent of American children are, or will soon be, members of such family units. Plainly, a new family system is emerging, one that differs greatly from the Biblical concept and creating what may indeed be an antichild spirit in the land.

Dr. James Dobson, widely recognized Christian psychologist and author of several books directed to parents and teachers, cautions that the future of the American family is very much in doubt. He points to these forces which are conspiring to undermine the traditional family: humanism, radio, television, movies, and the press—all with their godless philosophies, infidelity, homosexuality, atheism, and self-centered lifestyles.

For the purposes of this book and this chapter, I want to zero in on the two most important things I believe teenagers need today.

Moms Who Are There

Our troublesome economy has sent many moms back into the work force. In many of these situations it's not a choice but a practical necessity. This is not meant to make working moms feel guilty in that kind of a situation; on the other hand, there are mothers pursuing their career goals just for the sake of career and to acquire material possessions. The children of such dual-career parents are paying the price, as *U.S. News & World Report* and other responsible parties are warning, "in ways that range from simple neglect to outright abuse."

Scarcely a day goes by without media accounts of such abused and neglected children. Especially when you are a parent yourself, these stories make your heart ache. I find myself wondering what kind of teenagers these children will become if they ever make it to adolescence. Edward Weaver, director of the American Public Welfare Association, comments, "Parents are caught in a crunch of conflicting values. They value children, but they value other things as well, such as time for themselves, material goods, status and their careers. Given these conflicts, in a number of instances they neglect children or don't give them a fair shake."[2] At the time of this writing there are more than 47 million children under the age of 14 affected by this state of affairs.

One writer has stated that a Christian home should be like a womb, giving the growing embryo of a marriage a place to safely develop, a space to move and stretch, to cry and struggle, until finally the relationship is fully developed and mature.[3] Enlarge that metaphor to include the children, and you are confronted with the harsh reality that many children are being "aborted" from the protective care of parents, especially when the mother is working and is not there when they need her most. *And that "needing her most" is most of the time.*

A mother asked me, "Why is it that when I come home from work at night, about 9 o'clock, my 15-year-old son has every light on in the house, even in the closets, and he has both stereos going full blast, and all the radios on, two televisions on, and the microwave on with nothing in it? Why is everything in my home turned on, including my son?"

I told this mother the truth: "Your son is lonely. All the lights and the noise makes for companionship. He needs you.'' The rock stars and disc jockeys have literally been invited by teenagers to become a member of their family. A lot of teenagers can tell you more about the local disc jockey than about their grandparents. Moms and dads aren't there, for whatever reason, and the teenager needs them. Teenagers especially need moms who are there.

Adolescence is a time of questioning. Someone has called adolescence the parent's second chance. The adolescent has reached the stage where he has acquired some reasoning skills. If the parent is there—the mom available—this child, with proper parental support, can make intelligent decisions for himself.

Earl D. Wilson, Ph.D., Associate Professor of Clinical and Counseling Psychology at Western Conservative Baptist Seminary, Portland, Oregon, points up the necessity for parents to realize that things have changed. While we may not like to admit this, things do change from one generation to another. Biblical truth is timeless and changeless, so what we as parents have to do is demonstrate in positive ways that our values and beliefs are worth following and accepting. Remember, these teenagers don't like being *told* what to do or what is acceptable, but by being available to them you can interact intelligently with them. In this whole process he is receiving the input from you that is so necessary to his growth and understanding. But when you aren't there or are too busy playing catch-up on housework and all the other things that busy mothers have to do when you *are* home, then this child is going to get shortchanged. Later *you* will groan and ask, ''What did I do wrong?''

Dr. Wilson states, ''I believe that if you are reasonable in your demands, and positive in your attitudes, the positive statement of values will result in a sense of pride in the values and in being a part of the family….Clearly stating values, and establishing a family identity around these values, helps to develop a spirit of family comradeship.''[4]

This family comradeship is nurtured best when mom is there to help handle issues as they arise, to listen and counsel, to dialogue—talking with, not talking to or talking at one's teenager—and to show that she understands and cares. One psychologist referred to adolescence as the period of storm and stress which can bring immense frustration upon parents. One of the greatest barriers to good parent-teen relationships is lack of time involvement—unhurried time. "Teenagers get sick and tired of being rushed. I believe spending time with children during the teen years is more important than at any other time. Unfortunately, we often smother children as preschoolers and starve them during the teen years," states Earl Wilson. This father of five children, who is a practicing psychologist, explains that he and his wife decided to try to make themselves more available to their children, and have been amazed at the benefits. "If you are always rushing or trying to regiment their lives, they will withdraw. Be there when they get home from school. Be there when they return from the ball game. Be there when they win and be there when they lose....

"Think how degrading it is to be told that your parents are too busy to spend time with you. Teenagers are smart enough to know that busyness is a choice. If you are too busy to spend time with them, they know inside that you are choosing other things ahead of them....Time is money, but time is also the substance from which good relationships are built."[5]

One clinical psychologist tells of a young woman expecting her first child. She commented to a friend that she wasn't going to quit her job when the baby came, and that as soon as she came home from the hospital and rested up for a few days, she was going back to work full-time. She stated, "It's better for me to go back to work right away and for the baby-sitter to start out right away, *so the baby won't get attached to me.*" The psychologist telling this observed that in his kind of work you become quite accustomed to the unusual, but that he has not become totally numb to shocking examples of inhumanity in family life, and this really got to him.

The working mother is at a disadvantage. She has God-given priorities with her family that must be met. And she has the added responsibility of living up to the expectations placed upon her by virtue of being employed. Pulled in different directions, tired and overworked, she finds herself having to barter golden hours with her children for a paycheck that doesn't stretch to meet their needs. Proverbs 1:8,9 admonishes children to listen to their father's instruction, and not to forsake their mother's teaching. In order to impart that kind of teaching, a woman needs to be able to spend time in the Word of God building up her own spiritual life so that she can be the godly mother that her children need. She knows she needs to be available to them at any time, ready to help and teach them. She knows also that her discipline is a requisite. Proverbs 29:15 says that the rod of correction imparts wisdom, but a child left to himself disgraces his mother. Christian women today have become victimized by society and a system that is at odds with the Bible's teachings. The pressure that this lays upon her is heavy.

My urging to mothers is that they carefully weigh their priorities, that they enlist their husband's understanding and help as they face the realities of their particular situation, and that they endeavor to show their children the difference between needs and wants so that, if at all possible, they can remain at home available to them. The Proverbs 31 woman had her priorities straight. It appears that she was a working woman to some extent, but in the process she didn't neglect the needs of her household. "She watches over the affairs of her household and does not eat the bread of idleness. Her children arise and call her blessed; her husband also, and he praises her: 'Many women do noble things, but you surpass them all' " (verses 27-29).

Catherine Marshall LeSourd relates how her late husband, Peter Marshall, put women on a pedestal. But what he had to say rings true and is a beautiful portrait of what the good wife and mother can and should be when she is relying on the Lord to make her life abundant for her husband, their children, and even out beyond the family circle. Here is what Marshall said in *A Man Called Peter:* "Modern girls argue that they have to earn an income in order to establish a home, which would be impossible on their husband's income. That is sometimes the case, but it must always be viewed as a regrettable necessity, never as the normal or natural thing for a wife to have to do. The average woman, if she gives her full time to her home, her husband, her children...if she tries to understand her husband's work...to curb his egotism while, at the same time, building up his self-esteem, to kill his masculine conceit while encouraging all his hopes, to establish around the family a circle of friends...if she provides in the home a proper atmosphere of culture, of love of music, of beautiful furniture and of a garden...if she can do all this, she will be engaged in a life work that will demand every ounce of her strength, every bit of her patience, every talent God has given her, the utmost sacrifice of her love. It will demand everything she has and more. And she will find that for which she was created. She will know that she is carrying out the plan of God. She will be a partner with the Sovereign Ruler of the universe."[6]

Much has been written and said in recent years about the emancipation of women and of women's liberation from the restraints of enforced domination by men. Some needed reforms have been attained, but there have been unfortunate side results as well. There has come a blurring of mother-father and male-female roles that has harmful effects on children. From childhood right on through those all-important adolescent years, our children need the security that comes from knowing they have moms who are there. Moms traditionally have been the stabilizing force in the family. To abdicate that privilege and responsibility is something you will regret in years to come. Dr. Charles Swindoll, senior pastor of the First Evangelical Free Church in Fullerton, California, and much-appreciated author, speaks to the despair which so many parents feel after they've raised their children and the family nest is empty. He talks of the empty feeling in the hearts of those who feel they blew it. "You broke most of the rules, you failed the test, and you cannot go back and try again. The hurt deep within is guilt mixed with a loss of hope....

"The passage of Scripture that applies so perfectly to your situation is found in the little book of Joel. In a series of several verses toward the end of the second chapter, God promised hope to people whose crops, groves, and vineyards had been ruined by insects."[7] But in the midst of that hopeless condition, the voice of God penetrated. Swindoll points the reader to Joel 2:24-26, and in particular to God's promise, "I will make up to you for the years that the swarming locust has eaten." The analogy is the locust of parental neglect and insensitivity, the swarming insects of indifference or ignorance or impatience, or a host of other famines brought on by parental failure which has eaten away at the relationship with precious children. Swindoll encourages parents experiencing this kind of pain to take to their own hearts God's promise: "God is a Specialist in impossible situations. He is the Physician who can bring internal healing. He specializes in binding up fractured relationships and healing deep wounds and bruises that have existed for years."[8]

The response that God desires from parents is that they give of themselves (Isaiah 58:10). Swindoll says, "As a parent who has blown it, the best place to start is with an open, honest confession of failure before God and your children. That's the place to begin 'giving yourself.' "[9]

You are reading this book, no doubt, because you are a concerned parent, someone who probably still has children at home, and quite possibly teenagers with whom you are struggling and seeking answers. I would hope that if you are a mom, you would grasp the opportunity that God is holding out to you even now as you read these words, and that you would become an available mom to your children—a mom who is there when they need her the most.

Dads Who Are Willing To Lead

The second thing that I believe teenagers need is dads who are willing to lead. Dad must be the dreamer in the family, the visionary, the one who has the ability to look down the road, to lead the members of his household, and the one who brings a sense of destiny to his family.

An example of the distinction between men and women in this area of dads being visionaries and women being realists can be seen in the matter of finances. Mothers will worry and say, "I'm telling you, we've got problems." Men will throw back their shoulders and announce, "Hey, it's going to work out." But the balance is important—with too much reality you have depression, and with too much destiny you have fantasy. We need visionary dads and realist moms—dads willing and able to lead, and moms willing and able to follow, with each maintaining a realistic, hopeful outlook on life.

Dad's discipline is part of his leadership role. This doesn't mean that mothers don't discipline, but it does mean that fathers share the responsibility for meting out correction and discipline to their children. "Discipline your son, and he will give you peace; he will bring delight to your soul" (Proverbs 29:17).

Dr. Max Rafferty, while State Superintendent of Public Instruction in California, blamed "dropout parents" for much of today's juvenile delinquency. He said, "We've been soft when we should have been tough. Permissive when we should have been stingy. Noninvolved when we should have been up to our ears."

The book of Proverbs has much to teach us as parents about our responsibilities to our children. The one thing that we as fathers and mothers desire early in life from these children loaned to us by the Lord is obedience. It is a cardinal virtue. Proverbs tells us that a rebellious child will bring grief to his mother (10:1), sorrow to his father (17:21,25), and bitterness to his mother (17:25). A foolish son brings ruin to his father (19:13). He is a disgrace who brings shame to both his father and his mother (19:26).

In contrast, a wise son heeds his father's instruction and listens to wise counsel. That is a consistent theme throughout the book of Proverbs. Where does a child learn right behavior? The answer appears to be at the hands and from the lips of fathers who know how to discipline with care and love (Proverbs 13:24). An absentee father cannot accomplish for his children what a father at hand can do. But it isn't just traveling fathers who are guilty of absenteeism; in fact, some fathers whose work requires absences do a better job of fathering than those who are at home most of the time. Fathers who abdicate their responsibility to their wives and fail to assume the leadership role in their homes are contributing to the chaos that exists in their children's lives.

Obedience isn't an optional thing for children. God's order for families plainly teaches that children are to obey their parents in the Lord (Colossians 3:20; Ephesians 6:1,2). But parents are admonished to deal fairly and rightly with their children, showing tenderness and love. This is underscored in the Apostle Paul's instructions aimed specifically at fathers: "Fathers, do not exasperate your children; instead, bring them up in the training and instruction of the Lord" (Ephesians 6:4).

Discipline is a part of love. This is clearly shown in the book of Hebrews, where God is pictured as a Father who must sometimes punish his children: "My son, do not make light of the Lord's discipline, and do not lose heart when he rebukes you, because the Lord disciplines those he loves, and he punishes everyone He accepts as a son'' (Hebrews 12:5,6).

Rebellion has rightly been called the untamed tiger in every young life. We are told, ''Discipline your son in his early years while there is hope. If you don't you will ruin his life'' (Proverbs 19:18 TLB). This takes the strong hand of a father who knows where to draw the line between exasperating his children and training, instructing, and correcting them in the Biblically correct manner. Fathers and mothers need to talk together about the kind of punishment that fits the situations into which their children become involved. They need to do this before the child becomes a partner in something major, so that the child will learn early in life that misdeeds bring their own peculiar kind of reward at the hands of a father committed to leading his family in the ways of truth, honesty, and right living. Gordon MacDonald *(The Effective Father)* points out that imperceptive young fathers often fail to see that the time to make investments in their family is when the child is young. ''Big returns never happen in the future unless sizable investments are made in the present.''

Gordon MacDonald stresses that fatherhood is more than a biological function. It is also a process of what he so rightly calls effective leadership. ''Inside the perimeters of the family, it is the father who is required to create delicate conditions in which a child grows to be a man or woman, to attain the fullness of all that human potential that God has designed. Where those conditions do not exist, growth is retarded, and human beings fall far short of the heavenly objectives.

''Families without fathers who are effective leaders face constant trouble, just like other kinds of groups where leadership is in a vacuum.''[10] In both the Old and New Testaments we have descriptions and commandments about the leadership role of the male head of the household. ''...in a unique sort of way, God calls upon the man to be the family's governor, its accountable representative to make sure that God's laws are being followed, that the people in that family have every opportunity to experience all that their Creator intends for them to be.''[11] And we are reminded that when family leadership is effective, there is a sense of order and poise.

A word of caution is in order for the fathers reading this. To be an effective leader for your family is *not* to be a dictator. It does not mean that you are the "king of your castle" who lords it over all the members of your family, expecting everyone to wait on you and demanding that they acquiesce to your every whim and demand.

I have encountered teenagers who are being raised in homes like this. These are young people who can't wait to get out from under their parents' roof. I've also talked to the wives of dictator husbands— women who have lost all their fight and for whom daily living is a struggle just to survive. They are miserable. The children in such a home are sad-eyed and unhappy. Home is not a haven; it's a battleground. Many of these teenagers end up in trouble; often the girls will get pregnant, and there is experimentation with drugs. The family is in a mess.

Who is to blame when situations like this exist? There are no simple answers and easy formulas. Happy families don't just happen. In a time of instant everything, we want things to happen right now. Fathers must realize that children learn largely by example and that love, patience, unselfishness, and other godly qualities should be practiced as well as taught. "Disordered families create disordered communities. Thus, God has sovereignly chosen one person in a family to create and maintain the needed order."[12] In God's economy, that person is to be the father.

I am indebted to Gordon MacDonald for his comprehensive study on what it takes to be an effective father. He states that there is a positive and a negative thrust to a father's leadership. "In its positive sense, effective leadership is designed to bring people to maturity, to the ultimate reaches of their human potential. The leader searches out the conditions in which each person in his family can grow to be what God has made him to be. But in the negative perspective, effective leadership is the enforcement of order when there is unwillingness to fit into the process of relationships, an attitude that makes life miserable for everyone.

"The head of the home—like the shepherd in Psalm 23—carries a kind of rod and staff: the staff for rescue and pointing direction, the rod for discipline and enforcement. When both are capably used, there is stability in relationships and steady progress in growth. When both are unused or misused, there is drift and deterioration among the shepherd's sheep and the father's family."[13]

My cousin, David Wilkerson (especially known for his book *The Cross and Switchblade*), tells of the firm discipline he received at the hand of his father. He called it *woodshed therapy* and states, "I believe it's time for a woodshed revival!"

Larry Christenson (*The Christian Family*) reminds parents that if our chastisement is to resemble the chastisement of Christ, it must be righteous. "Firmness and uniformity must prevail in it. There must not be harshness at one time and then indulgence at another, in the same case. It must be proportioned to the importance of the fault.... We must look to the moral issue....

"As Christians, we live under the discipline of Christ. He disciplines us severely as often as we need it. His object is not to spare us pain, but to surely slay the will of the flesh. Yet He disciplines us with moderation. He does not afflict us willingly. And as soon as He sees that we bow down and acknowledge our faults, He comes to us with consolation; he lets us feel how great is His kindness! So He deals with us, and so we ought to deal with our children."[14]

It is an awesome responsibility to be a parent. But we have been given adequate instructions and we have been promised supernatural help. That help comes as we turn our lives over to the Lord and as the Holy Spirit is given the reins of our lives. If you are going to be the kind of father your teenager needs, then you will be a man who is allowing his life to be transformed daily, touched by the power of Jesus Christ.

It is said that the average father in the United States spends 38 minutes per week talking to his children. When you consider that there are 1440 minutes in each day, you realize how little of himself the average father is giving to his offspring. It has been pointed out that "you may not be able to do anything about your ancestors, but you can do something about your descendants." But spending only 38 minutes per week with a child isn't going to allow much time for "doing something about one's descendants."

Jesus is to be our example. Jesus spent hours every day talking to *His* Father. John 17 is a great example of that. Fathers need to spend meaningful talking time with their children, and when they do, and when they have preceded that by talking to *their heavenly Father,* then I can tell you, on the authority of the Word of God, that their life and the lives of their offspring will be blessed.

This is what it means to be what your teenager needs—a dad who is willing to lead.

NOTES

1. "Our Neglected Kids," in *U.S. News & World Report,* Aug. 9, 1982, p. 54.
2. Ibid.
3. Jill Briscoe, *Fight for the Family* (Grand Rapids: Zondervan Publishing House, 1981), p. 22.
4. Earl D. Wilson, *You Try Being a Teenager* (Portland: Multnomah Press, 1982), pp. 117-118.
5. Ibid., pp. 15-16.
6. Catherine Marshall, *A Man Called Peter.*
7. Charles R. Swindoll, *You and Your Child* (Nashville: Thomas Nelson Publishers, 1977), p. 158.
8. Ibid., p. 158.
9. Ibid., p. 159.
10. Gordon MacDonald, *The Effective Father* (Wheaton: Tyndale Publishing House, 1977), p. 15.
11. Ibid., p. 16.
12. Ibid., p. 23.
13. Ibid.
14. Larry Christenson, *The Christian Family* (Minneapolis: Bethany Fellowship, 1970), pp. 107-08.

4

The Nature and Needs of Junior-High Young People

The discerning heart seeks knowledge.

Proverbs 15:14

What are the basic root problems that young people are facing today that are contributing to some of the problems in society? Young people, I believe, are existential: they would rather *experience* something than have to take the time to think through the possible ramifications of their choices.

Many young people today don't like reading (a lot of them *can't* read well, thanks to the education they have received), and they struggle with all the implications of that. Kids today are largely media-oriented. It's boom, boom, boom—hit them with this, hit them with that. Keep moving, moving, moving. They are accustomed to change, with segments of television programs constantly changing. Advertisers spend small fortunes for a 30-second commercial to keep kids' attention.

The largest buyers of record albums are young girls ages 11 to 13. The music industry is geared to a young market. Everything is geared to the senses and emotions. It is all experience-oriented. If it feels good, buy it or do it, but don't try to explain it.

This evens shows up in church. The experiences of those whose lives have been transformed are written about and talked about, and these individuals are catapulted into the forefront. The more bizarre their experiences before coming to Christ, the more they are exploited. This is not to condemn all exciting testimonies, but it is to show how existential we have become.

How do we best understand the moving of the Holy Spirit in our individual lives? Is it not by reading and meditating upon the Word of God and spending time in prayer? Do you know how difficult it is to get people to do that on a consistent basis? It is even *more* difficult to motivate young people to do this regularly. Adults as well as adolescents don't want to take the time to learn about God and thus come to understand His ways, but they sure like to feel that He is working in their lives. Because we are so feeling-oriented, we would rather go by our feelings than by knowledge gained through developing a close communion and fellowship with the Lord.

Secondly, young people are being raised in what I call a "dehumanized society." This generation of children has been raised to believe that science and technology provide all the answers to man's struggles. They have also been raised to believe that by drastically changing the social and political structure of society we would have a more just and equal world in which to live. That hasn't worked either. There are more inequities than ever before. The "haves" and the "have nots" seem to be farther apart than ever.

A third thing that young people have been raised to believe is that by dismantling repressive taboos of the past they will enjoy far more freedom and self-realization. The 1970s will be remembered as the decade that waged war against the family—when antifamily values were thrown at our kids by educators, authors, and sociologists. Alternate lifestyles have been touted as highly desirable—such things as teenage sex, adultery, homosexuality, and easy divorce. Traditional family values have largely been scorned and labeled repressive.

Over and over again, in one way or another, our young people have been told that conventional marriage represents a major and unnecessary reduction in sexual pleasure. One writer declared that if thwarted sexual desires are, as many "authorities" maintain, among the chief causes of emotional disturbance, then the message is glaringly clear: sexual freedom is where it's at. The idea presented was that personal freedom is what everyone needs, regardless of age or sex, and that to follow a set of rigid prescriptions throughout life is neither possible nor desirable. While marriage would continue to be a legal and socially acceptable institution, nonmarital and modified-marital relationships should also be equally legal and socially acceptable. This writer stated that at whatever age the sex drive is strongest, as well as at all other ages, the individual should have the right to unlimited sexual expression, provided only that his behavior does not infringe upon the rights of others.[1]

This writer, as well as others writing in a similar vein, acknowledged that marriage and monogamistic ideals still hold sway in this country, and so premarital and extramarital sex are regarded almost automatically as infringements on either the rights of specific other people or on the whole structure of public morality. He wrote that 80 percent of the societies of the world permit multiple sexual relationships, and he strongly suggested that our society would not be risking ruin if it became equally tolerant. "Marriage, for most people, has outlived its usefulness and is doing more harm than good," stated this professor of psychology.[2]

It should be understood that this kind of writing and teaching has been common across the country, and it is this kind of society in which your children have to interact with other people. So many parents, I find, have been living such sheltered lives that they are hardly aware of what's been going on out there in the world. Is it any wonder that they find it difficult to communicate with their young sons and daughters?

The above-mentioned writer, representative of others, argues that children should be placed in child-care institutions. "It is to be supposed that the principles of ethical, productive and happy living will be learned more readily when children are free of the insecurities, engendered chiefly by parents, that ordinarily obstruct the internalization of these modes of thought.* The children would also be exposed to the teachings of the various religions, along with the rationales for the atheistic and agnostic positions. Those who wish to embrace a particular religion would be perfectly free to do so."[3]

Lest the reader think this writer is not characteristic of the writing and thinking of many others, let me hasten to explain that a trip by you to any library will quickly unearth others saying the same kinds

---

* The previous sentence had explained that children would learn what used to be called the American way of life—values, such as honesty, fair play, cooperation, and tolerance, that have been advocated so strongly (in literature, and supposedly in traditional family homes), "but taught so poorly."

of things. Our children have consistently been brainwashed into believing that for far too long freedom in this country has not meant free choice, that there are more liberating lifestyles out there than they have been led to believe in their family situation, and that as long as they continue to believe everything their parents say they will be emotionally handicapped. "...a thorough overhauling of many of our social institutions—economic, religious, and political—must be undertaken if human happiness and dignity are to have a fighting chance for survival....It is possible that a 'perfect' society will never exist. But a vastly improved society *can* exist—if, and only if, enough dedicated men and women are able to envisage, and willing to work toward, its actualization," this writer concludes.[4]

This kind of thinking has permeated society. Is it any wonder that we have seen an erosion of traditional family values? As I go across the country I observe the trauma this has inflicted on families, especially young people, and I am committed to warning parents and their children about what I see happening.

As all this relates to junior-high young people in the three areas of their physical, emotional, and spiritual needs, here are some things to specifically be aware of.

The Explosive Years

Physically these are incredibly explosive years for junior-highers. One day, as this child steps over the threshhold from 12 to 13, you suddenly find yourself wondering where the years went. What happened? The child is coming into puberty—legally described generally as age 14 for boys and 12 for girls. But children differ, and I've known one boy who had things start happening to him at age ten! He walked up to me while I was on an Alaska speaking tour and said, "Mr. Wilkerson, I'm 13. I've been sleeping with a girl friend off and on for a year."

When a junior-higher walks up to you, all you can see is arms and legs that never stop moving. They trip easily. I've seen these kids walking when boom, the next thing you know they've landed flat on their face. "What happened?" you ask, and they respond, "I was walking."

At this time in their lives their bodies are growing faster than their brains. Girls at this age are wondering why they're looking down at the boys their age. Girls shoot up faster than the boys. Girls in particular act and appear older than their years. Both the fellows and the girls have a short attention span.

Primarily the physical development of the junior-high young person has three aspects: 1) general physical growth; 2) sexual maturation; and 3) development of physical appearance and abilities. All of this reflects on their behavior, which can be described as turbulent and unpredictable. Changes in their bodily proportions make them feel awkward, and they appear restless.

If you were to watch me do a school assembly for these kids you'd probably think I was totally out of my mind. I'm walking from one end of the stage to the other; I'm up and down the aisles. I would appear to be out of control, just like they are. But I've got to hold their attention. You see, the back of their laps won't endure too long, and neither does their mind stay engaged too well! In fact, one study came out with a startling statistic that said the average attention span for a junior-higher is only four minutes!

It is vital that parents try to understand what kids at this age are going through with regard to their physiques (boys) and figures (girls). Overnight they can outgrow their clothes (or so it seems, mothers tell me). They are very self-conscious about the way they look; they haven't become accustomed to some of their new physical developments and endowments.

More than one parent has shared with me that they have often felt they were on a collision course with their children with regard to the way they feel they look. Some mothers find it difficult to believe that their "little girl" isn't a little girl anymore and is ready for a different look. Parents need to be especially sensitive to this physical growth and its problems and be ready to offer the emotional support the child so desperately needs in order to accept himself or herself.

In the area of sexual maturing, there is a relationship between sexuality and responsibility that needs to be taught, but not taught by threats or fear. Earl Wilson (*You Try Being a Teenager*) reminds parents that sexuality is a gift from God that needs to be accepted with joy and celebration, not fear and trepidation. I'll have more to say on this subject in a later chapter. Of first importance, however, is to recognize the need to educate your own child about his/her sexuality; don't leave it up to public schools and/or the child's peers. Help your child to understand the need to make good choices related to his/her sexuality *before* bad choices have been made.

In the development of his physical appearance and abilities, recognize that your child is experiencing some rejection from his peers. This is closely related to his emotional development. He is in uncharted territory, and it's scary.

Low Self-Esteem

The child's emerging identity is aligned with the way he feels about the way he looks and the skills he feels he possesses or lacks. He may feel he doesn't measure up to your expectations—perhaps he's been turned down for the basketball team. Or your daughter didn't make it as a cheerleader. Earl Wilson cautions about adding your rejection to what they already feel they are receiving from their peers, and also what they already feel about themselves.

These are critical transition periods in their young lives, and they need the support that parents can best provide. They need direction and they need your availability; on the other hand, they don't want you hovering over them providing blueprints, as it were, for their every move. This is the time when you begin to equip them to do some thinking on their own and, as they show that they can make good decisions, they need praise, affirmation, encouragement, and reassurance. Parents can provide the intellectual stimulation that will motivate their junior-high child to do some serious thinking on his own. This in itself will bolster his self-esteem. Keep good books and magazines around, encourage your child to watch good educational programs on TV, and then talk about the things they've read and seen.

Remember Jesus' youth? The temple teachers were amazed at His understanding and His answers. Yes, He was God in the flesh, but He was also Jesus the son of Mary. We read that He grew in wisdom and stature, and in favor with God and men (Luke 2:52). It is noteworthy that Luke, the physician, should thus describe Jesus' adolescence in this way.

The same thing was said of the boy Samuel (see 1 Samuel 2:26). We need to allow our children to grow up, and preadolescence, these junior-high years, are all-important in starting them out on that right path. Try remembering your own turbulent early adolescent years when your hair was totally unmanageable and when you woke up one morning—the day of that important first date—only to discover 37 new zits on your face. And remember, there's no tomorrow for them at this age. They only know how to live for today. All they have is right now. An immediate predicament looms as a Grand Canyon impossibility that will thwart them for the rest of their lives.

Spiritual Development

Spiritually, the junior-high young person is a dreamer. Many of you reading this began dreaming about what you are today when you were in junior high. Wise parents seek to discern the special gifts and abilities that God has uniquely put into their child. These parents don't try to pour their child into a preconceived mold of what *they* think the child should be or do, but they are tuned to what *God* is doing in that child's life. Pray for perception so that you can be a wise counselor to your child.

When I was in junior high I felt a call from God into the ministry, and I never backed off from that vision. My parents knew of my dream and didn't stifle that God-given vision. Some parents look at their children and the glazed look in the eyes of this young adolescent, and accuse the child of too much daydreaming. What a mistake! They may have several dreams and change their mind about what they want to do or be, but that's okay. This is all a part of their spiritual development as they seek to be in tune with God in their own lives. I would imagine that young David spent many hours in that kind of reflective thinking as he tended his father's sheep on the Judean hillside.

Remember, your junior-higher is still a child to some extent. His mind is vulnerable. He is also gullible and can be easily lured into wrong thinking. He wants to believe. He also wants to believe in people. However, the hypocrisy he has seen in some adults (and in some parents) has made him somewhat wary, and rightfully so.

Still, junior-highers cling to some idealistic notions, though idealism among teenagers seems to be on the wane. *The World Almanac and Book of Facts* polled 2000 eighth-grade American pupils to learn which persons they most admire and would want to be like when they grow up. Asked to name their top 30 heroes, their leading role model turned out to be Burt Reynolds. He was followed by such names as Richard Pryor, Alan Alda, Steve Martin, Robert Redford, and the late John Belushi.

Half of these students polled were girls, but only five women appeared on the list, and they were all actresses, models, or pop singers. Sadly, there wasn't a single name on the list who wasn't an entertainer or a sports figure. No statesmen. No scientists. No authors. No painters, musicians, sculptors, architects, doctors, lawyers, theologians, religious persons, or even astronauts.

These were young people ready to enter high school, but not one of them chose to model himself or herself upon someone who has made a real or lasting contribution to the world. I think it can be stated with some degree of accuracy that surveys leave more questions than answers. We wonder what is wrong. Who is at fault? Why this disenchantment and disillusionment with men and women whom we as adults would consider more acceptable role models?

Syndicate writer Sydney Harris points out that the heroes and heroines of our youth today are not people who have done big things, but people who have made it big. Our adolescents have absorbed the values of their parents to a great extent, and it would appear that the cult of success has overtaken them.

Have you looked at the posters on the walls in your child's room? I've seen them—their heroes are rock stars, the phony media fantasy hypes. Even the athletes of today don't present the image they once did. According to the *Los Angeles Times* nearly 70 percent of the NBA (National Basketball Association) players were using cocaine. I urge parents to help their children identify people within the Christian community whom they can look up to and respect. Our adolescents need Christian heroes and heroines. More specifically, older adolescents are looking for leaders.

Parents who wish to promote spiritual development in their adolescents (and every parent should want to do this) need to remember the Scriptural warning about not being a stumbling block: "But whoever causes one of these little ones who believe in Me to stumble, it is better for him that a heavy millstone be hung around his neck, and that he be drowned in the depth of the sea" (Matthew 18:6 NASB).

The first leader the adolescent should want to follow is his own parents. Mothers and fathers who have become accustomed through the years to dropping their children off at Sunday school and/or church, but not staying themselves, have set a poor example. In a 1981 study by Nurses Christian Fellowship of 263 churched youth ages 13 to 18, 79.5 percent felt that their religious beliefs were the same as, or similar to, their parents' beliefs. Only 12.5 percent held very different beliefs, and most of those thought their own beliefs were stronger (for example, "My parents don't go to church" or "My parents only use God's name in curse words").[5]

But teenagers have always been quick to recognize inconsistencies between what adults teach and how they actually live and behave. As already stated, they can become easily disillusioned by hypocrisy. This has been pointed out by psychologist Arthur Jersild, who quotes studies which indicate that adolescents react in one of two ways to conflict between what parents say and do. The teenager will either cling desperately to a formal acceptance of ideals and religious convictions or else become cynical and reject his parents' religious beliefs.[6]

It is at this time in teenagers' lives that the peer group can become more significant than parents in influencing values. But it has also been shown, and many parents can attest to this, that values taught in earlier years will probably be maintained later on. As Proverbs teaches, if we are diligent in training our children in the way they should go, when they are older they will not depart from it (see Proverbs 22:6).

Children who come from homes where there is a lot of dissension often become adolescents who are distrustful of all adults. Adolescents like this have trouble seeing the church in a positive light; they are less likely to affirm faith or to make a commitment, and they do not have a great deal of hope in their young lives. There is a sense of hopelessness which they convey, of pessimism and a gloomy outlook. (I will have more to say on this in discussing the spiritual nature and needs of senior-high young people.)

In Summary

Remembering the vulnerability of junior-highers, parents will want to do all they possibly can to help their children through these tumultuous years. Dr. James Dobson, one of the most widely read and highly respected psychologists of our time, warns parents of the emotional conflicts—the fears, doubts, and pressures—that they will experience. At this gateway to older adolescence they need all the help they can get. On the other hand, they must be released to develop independence and maturity, or else they will rise up later angry and guilty, rejecting our bondage and interference. Dobson says, "Hold on with an open hand." Emancipate them slowly with Christian grace, the kind of God-given wisdom that your heavenly Father will supply, maintaining love and authority in proper balance. We are reminded in Scripture that the tongue of the righteous is as choice silver (Proverbs 10:20 NASB), that the mouth of the righteous flows with wisdom (Proverbs 10:31 NASB), and that the lips of the righteous bring forth what is acceptable (Proverbs 10:32 NASB).

NOTES

1. Lawrence Casler, "Permissive Matrimony: Proposals For the Future," in *The Humanist*, Mar./Apr. 1974, p. 6.
2. Ibid., p. 4.
3. Ibid., p. 7.
4. Ibid., p. 8.
5. Judith Allen Shelly, *The Spiritual Needs of Children* (Downers Grove, Illinois: Inter-Varsity Press, 1982), p. 55.
6. Ibid., p. 56.

5

The Nature and Needs of Senior-High Young People

Blessings crown the head of the righteous.
Proverbs 10:6

Linus is talking to Lucy: "It's starting to rain." Lucy holds out her hands to make sure, then adds with characteristic sarcasm, "It figures. It always rains on our generation."

Her attitude is typical of many adolescents struggling with their identity in a world they feel has turned sour on them. What they fail to realize is that it rains on our generation, too. One father, writing in the front of a Charles Schulz book which he gave to his daughter, called this to her attention and added, "Don't let it [the rain] ever stop your parade."

How can we as parents walk through the sunshine *and* the rain in this parade called life *with* our senior-high adolescents, and help them become well-adjusted, able to survive without becoming cynical or expecting too much from a world that is not all sweetness and light?

The Coming-Out Years

Dr. James Dobson, in describing this time of life, speaks of these years as coming in with a pimple and going out with a beard. They are the flirtatious years, when girls begin to powder and boys begin to puff. Fears, jeers, and tears are representative of these tumultuous youth, with parents who quake and tremble as they watch their children stumble through.

Physically, these are the coming-out years. The adolescent has matured physically. Every time I drive onto a school campus I experience a degree of shock. "What happened to high school girls?" I asked a pastor accompanying me one day. "I mean, they all look alike—you know, candidates for Miss America." There's not going to be a whole lot more budding after the age of 17.

And the fellows—the macho image must be perpetuated. My dad spent at least 38 minutes daily just telling me to get out of the bathroom. Things really haven't changed much. Deodorant and mouthwash—we can't live without them. Dressing up the physical frame is all-important for the guys as well as the gals. Girls aren't the only ones who need blow dryers, acne cover-up, and cologne. Primping takes a big toll of their time in the adolescent years.

The moodiness which is characteristic of adolescents can to a large degree be traced to their preoccupation with the way they look. They are adjusting to the physical changes in their bodies, even as parents are struggling to get used to the metamorphosis. When they aren't satisfied with the way they look, they can go into a blue funk lasting for days. In a cartoon depicting two adolescents talking together about the first day of school, in answer to the question "How do you feel facing the first day of school?" the girl responds, "Supremely confident." The fellow says, "Oh, say—you have a speck of lint on your lapel..." and the girl goes into a tizzy. She becomes irrational, sheds tears, and goes into a panic. It's raining on her generation!

An Emotional Seesaw

Emotionally, high-schoolers' self-esteem has changed from their junior high days. Either their confidence has built and reached a peak bordering on arrogance or else they may go in the extreme direction of being more shy and introverted than they were in junior high. Somewhere along these maturing years they either lost all confidence or gained a tremendous amount of it. They are on an emotional seesaw.

Seldom at this stage in life do you see a young person who is emotionally mature; usually the needed balance is lacking. Either they're supercool or they're Miss or Mr. Wallflower. They've been reading and hearing the garbage that maintains you have to be beautiful, sharp, and handsome—and possess incredible wit—to be successful and liked. There appears to be no room for Mr. In-between or Miss Average.

The competition is keen, resulting in feelings of isolation and pressure. Self-esteem has definitely changed—either it's rising or further depreciating. Parents who fail to recognize this, not understanding what is happening, focus on the frightening tension rather than giving the child the understanding and support he so desperately needs. To draw out the adolescent's feelings is difficult; he tends to become introspective, thinking his own thoughts and writing secrets in diaries or in notes to members of the opposite sex.

This is a troublesome time of life. The emotional conflict is difficult for the teens to handle. One day they are madly in love with someone; the next day they hate that person with an equal intensity. But love is definitely in the air. The attraction to the opposite sex is strong. These emotions dictate their actions and reactions. Failing to understand these fickle emotional feelings, the adolescent in and out of love experiences depression, anger, betrayal, and a host of letdown-type reactions. "What does he think?" "What does she think?" "Is he going to call?" That's all that's on their minds. Homework suffers, as well as relationships with other people. Lovesickness has overtaken them.

One of the major problems in our world today is that we don't understand love without strings attached, and this wrong concept of love often gains its greatest foothold in these adolescent years. Real love—not just turning on your feelings for someone else—is the answer to life's woes. I'm talking about love based on personal choice and commitment, love rooted in the kind of unconditional love that God extended to humankind through His only Son. That kind of love is explained best in 1 Corinthians 13:4-7, which can rightly be called the heart-of-love chapter: "Love is patient, love is kind. It does not envy, it does not boast, it is not proud. It is not rude, it is not self-seeking, it is not easily angered, it keeps no record of wrongs. Love does not delight in evil but rejoices with the truth. It always protects, always trusts, always hopes, always perseveres." The most basic need that any of us has is to be loved. The adolescent who receives this agape-type love in the home is less likely to seek love and attention in unsatisfying romantic-love attachments with members of the opposite sex.

According to Earl Wilson, teenagers report that they know they are loved when one or more of the following conditions are met by their parents: when parents work to provide for them; when parents listen and don't lecture; when parents treat them like they have brains; when parents do things for them without constantly reminding them of the sacrifices they're making; when parents treat them like adults; and when parents allow them some freedom.[1] I agree that this is not an all-inclusive list, but it does provide some insights into loving teenagers.

One of the most important things that parents can communicate to their adolescents relates to priorities that will help stabilize their emotional life. The first priority is a right relationship with God. Who is Lord of their life? God will not coerce anyone to love Him. "I love those who love Me, and those who seek Me find Me" (Proverbs 8:17) are not words from a God who forces His love on His children.

Parents must communicate their love to their adolescent by saying "I love you" in both words and deeds. Many adults I talk to tell me they don't ever remember their moms and dads telling them verbally that they truly cared. They may have provided a roof over their heads, food on the table, and clothes on their back, but they failed to open their arms to embrace their hungry-for-love, emotionally starved teenager. Many teenagers tell me they have parents who do not spend time with them nor do they convey words of endearment that in any way demonstrate their love. Is it any wonder that such adolescents rebel and participate in drugs, drinking, sex, and other activities that break the hearts of their parents? Kids such as this easily become part of a group. They are seeking to fill this void in their lives.

The key to surviving the emotional experiences of these adolescent years, as Dobson advises, is to lay the proper foundation and then face these years with courage and certainty. There will be a certain amount of rebellion, conflict, and friction, but it can produce a healthy relationship between parents and their children when parents do not panic. Accept what you cannot always understand in your adolescent, allow him to make mistakes and to have his emotional ups and downs, and encourage him to express his feelings. Work to develop mutual respect; remember that love is not earned and that we can't buy our children's affection. Respect your child's abilities and plans and his need for privacy. Earl Wilson cautions about playing cops and robbers, as it were, and spying on your teenager or mistrusting him. Don't be surprised if your teenager turns to his peers rather than you if in these and other areas you have let him down. Compliment your adolescent; show him that you respect his abilities and ideas. If he can see that he is progressing and maturing, he will feel more positively about himself. This helps to develop confidence.

"Balanced growth by the adolescent is best encouraged by the presence of parental guidelines. Just as a plant grows the straightest when attached to a stake, so a teenager needs the stability of straight guidelines from the parents. Teenagers feel more secure when they know the boundaries of the playing field. They will disagree with the boundaries, and in some instances will ask that the boundaries be changed, but they do like boundaries," writes Earl Wilson.[2] He emphasizes that guidelines are not shackles to prevent growth. Such guidelines can only help to stabilize the fluctuating emotions of the adolescent. Just as God does not force His love on us, nor His guidelines, even so parents need to let their teenager know that rules are meant to be followed. There are consequences to pay when we turn our backs on God, and there is a price to pay when our children make wrong choices. All of this is part of the rounding-out of their character and can contribute to emotional stability.

Spiritually Speaking

Where do our children learn absolutes? Where should they first be learning and hearing spiritual truth? The only religious instruction that some children receive is an hour on Sunday morning at Sunday school. (Some don't even get that!) Is this all that *your* adolescent has received throughout his young life? If so, then don't be surprised at the direction his teenage years take. In 2 Timothy 1:5 we are given a glimpse of what teenager Timothy received. The Apostle Paul is writing: "I have been reminded of your sincere faith, which first lived in your grandmother Lois and in your mother Eunice and, I am persuaded, now lives in you also."

What a tremendous heritage for any child to receive at any age! It's never too early or too late to begin. Timothy's godly training prepared him for living in an ungodly world—the same kind of ungodly world (perhaps even more so) that our teenagers face today.

If you follow along in this book of 2 Timothy, you see that the learning Timothy received resulted in knowledge and in turn to personal conviction. "But as for you, continue in what you have learned and have become convinced of, because you know those from whom you learned it, and how from infancy you have known the holy Scriptures, which are able to make you wise for salvation through faith in Christ Jesus" (2 Timothy 3:14,15).

Dr. Charles Swindoll in referring to these verses explains that wisdom is simply looking at life from God's point of view—applying Biblical principles to everyday life.

It is of utmost importance that our senior-highers receive spiritual truth from those whom they know and can trust (reread the above verse). I have a reason for emphasizing this point. Adolescents, I have discovered, are unwilling to criticize another person's beliefs. "Well, so what if he wants to believe that!" So what if he's a Hindu, a Christian Scientist, etc.! When they are not firmly grounded themselves, they can easily be led astray. We've seen this in recent years as thousands of young people have been led off into various cults. We've read and heard accounts of how such kids have been deprogrammed. How were they lured away to begin with? It is safe to say that they did not have the conviction which Paul said young Timothy possessed.

Because adolescence is the time of questioning, the senior-higher needs to be well-grounded in the faith of his parents. Parents who talk about their beliefs and demonstrate their faith are setting a good example for their children. I can remember hearing both my mom and dad praying aloud consistently and mentioning our names. Sometimes it was early in the morning and sometimes late at night. I've seen them weep for us, crying out to the Lord for our specific needs. This had a strong subconscious effect on my life. Not only did those prayers touch the throne of God, but they touched and reached my heart.

Young adolescents are reading their parents and other adults like a book. This shouldn't frighten us; it should only make us more alert, aware, and sensitive to their spiritual needs. God doesn't need us to exaggerate for Him, but our enthusiasm for the things of the Lord can have a rub-off effect.

We should deal with our teenagers' questions openly and honestly. The Holy Spirit in us can be counted upon to respond, showing us from the Bible what we need to pass on to them. When they have left the security of the family nest and are confronted with the challenges in the world and from other students and from professors, they will be much less vulnerable (see 1 Peter 3:15).

Rebellion is a trademark of teenagers. Why? Because for the most part at this age there is so little genuine repentance. True repentance has to do with a cleaning out of the heart. The heart is the place where the will is seated. What is the will? "John, take the trash out." It's a simple request. Does John do it? Chances are, if he's like a lot of adolescents, he simply ignores your request.

When I was 17 I thought I had all the answers; in fact, I knew that I knew everything there was to know about anything. Today I know that I'm greatly uninformed and that even a lifetime of studying and learning will leave me woefully ignorant of all there is to be known. Paul's charge to Timothy is one that young people need to be reminded to today (see 1 Timothy 6:3-5). The apostle warned this young man to flee false doctrines; to avoid controversies, malicious talk, evil suspicions, and friction; and to not let other people rob him of the truth. The Apostle Paul cautioned against the love of money and against wandering from the faith: "Flee from all this, and pursue righteousness, godliness, faith, love, endurance and gentleness. Fight the good fight of the faith" (1 Timothy 6:11,12a).

Teenagers like a challenge. If the Christianity to which they are exposed is boring, the chances are that they might leave it. When I was in the youth ministry in a pastoral position, I never told kids it was going to be fun. I always told them it was going to be tough! "Probably most of you won't make it," I'd say. "You wanna bet!" they'd respond. "We can too!"

After hearing me preach to a group of high school kids, one man said, "Wilkerson, are you trying to scare people out of hell?" I looked at him, thought for just a quick moment, and replied, "No, I'm daring young people into heaven. They want a challenge." Of course they do; they've got so much energy. They like to be told something is next to impossible. They feel they are invincible. So when someone tells them they shouldn't do something, or that something is tough or impossible, their reaction is, "Let me at it—I'll show 'em." If we are going to reach them for Christ, then let's tell them it's a challenge, that it's not easy to serve God.

Young Timothy was told to guard what had been entrusted to his care, and to turn away from godless chatter and the opposing ideas of what is falsely called knowledge (1 Timothy 6:20). Paul never once spared speaking the truth to this young man. He never led him to believe that it was going to be easy to live for Christ. "In fact, everyone who wants to live a godly life in Christ Jesus will be persecuted," Paul told him (2 Timothy 3:12). He advised Timothy to keep his head in all situations, and to endure hardship (4:5).

Older adolescents are usually not looking for heroes anymore. Their heroes have let them down, but they are still searching for a leader. They don't want to fantasize anymore; they need someone who will point the way. Fathers who demonstrate leadership in the home will be highly respected by their sons and daughters.

When you put leadership through the teenager's test, and leadership comes through tried and true, you will have yourself a lifelong loyalist. They want their leaders to demonstrate nonprejudice. Tension builds when they sense that their parents and/or other adults are being judgmental. They can quickly become very pessimistic, and this leads to purposelessness. They need examples of concern, of caring adults, of real compassion. The world shows them primarily competition in areas of fame, wealth, and success.

Teenagers can be very hard on themselves. One fellow wrote me and said, "I get so down on myself that I start taking it out on my parents. I feel so guilty. Can you tell me how to get out of this mess?" I complimented the writer and told him that one of the hardest things to do is to admit failure. But then I urged him to stop focusing on his mistakes. "Get your eyes off the problem and onto the solution," I urged. The solution, of course, is Jesus. (Read Psalm 27:13.) Here are the steps I gave him to help him keep focusing on Jesus. 1) Be honest with your parents. Tell them what you told me (See Proverbs 1:8.)

2) Share your testimony with someone at school every day. This will help you to maintain a Christian example. (See Romans 1:16.) 3) Always remember that God is stronger than the devil. The temptations will not stagger you like they once did if you remember this. (See 1 John 4:4.)

All of us make mistakes and do spiritual battle. This is a part of the growth process. Teenagers, however, easily allow themselves to be buried by past failure, not comprehending that this is a lifelong battle.

Nurses Christian Fellowship (NCF) surveyed adolescents and found 98.5 percent expressing a strong belief in God. This is in contrast to the Gallup Poll finding, which showed the general youth population disillusioned with the institutional church. What it does point up is that teenagers are not giving up on God, but some of them are giving up on the church. They are watching the church and its leaders with a wary eye. Half the teenagers surveyed by NCF said that their beliefs about God had changed since becoming a teenager. Eighty-one percent of those said their faith had become stronger, more mature, or more relevant. To what did they attribute the change? It was catechetical instruction, Bible study, youth camps and programs, and the influence of peers and Christian leaders. Noticeably lacking was parental influence.

This same NCF poll showed 72 percent of those surveyed attending church services often. Only 6 percent never attended. And most continued to attend Sunday school and participate in church activities during high school. What were their reasons given for church involvement?

63 percent because they enjoy it
49 percent because they see friends there
31 percent because of a personal sense of duty
26 percent because of their parents' example
20 percent because their parents made them attend.[3]

Swindoll (*You and Your Child*) emphasizes the father's role in teaching his sons to be sensitive to God. What he is saying is equally applicable to daughters. He maintains that our children will rise up and call us blessed if we develop a tender spirit in them toward the Lord. He asks the question "Why?" and answers it by stating that this will save the child untold hours of grief and heartache. He points to Proverbs 3:11,12 which talks about sensitivity to instruction: "My son, do not reject the discipline of the Lord or loathe His reproof; for whom the Lord loves He reproves, even as a father the son in whom he delights'' (NASB).

How can we tip the scale so that our adolescent sons and daughters can point to our influence in their lives as being the most influential force in shaping their beliefs about God? It will require the investment of our personal time if we are to impart values and godly principles to our children. Dr. Charles Swindoll suggests three specifics in this area: 1) teach them how to respond to your own counsel; 2) help them see the value of other people's correction; and 3) share a few shadows from your own lives—insights from where you have failed and paid dearly for refusing to listen to God, and then convey the benefits of maintaining a sensitive spirit, as opposed to being hot and cold.[4]

I would urge parents to develop relationships with their sons and daughters that are meaningful and memorable and will last forever. I treasure the relationship that my parents developed with me. They provided a warehouse of memories and meaningful experiences that I have built my life on and will continue to use in the work that God has entrusted to me, as well as in my own family relationships. The greatest job that we as parents have is to nurture our children in the things of the Lord. If we major on this, someday we can look back upon our lives with few regrets. Ask yourself these questions: What needs does my child have? How am I helping him? Does the uniqueness of his or her needs demand something extra from me at this present time? If so, what kind of attention is required? How can I best fulfill my responsibility before the Lord and my family?

In Summary

In helping our teenagers become mature persons, with a secure identity and a strong reliance on God, here are some things they would like us to remember:

> Try to understand us.
> Listen when we talk and try to communicate with us.
> Give us more freedom.

Trust us and respect us; don't assume that all teenagers are bad.

Set limits and discipline us fairly when we disobey.

Show love constantly and consistently.

Don't preach at us—it only turns us off.

Give encouragement and affirmation when we do things right.

Don't condemn us and make us feel guilty.

Spend time with us.

Pray for us and with us.

Be good examples for us.

Lead (don't push) us in the right way.

Don't yell and make threats; they only cause rebellion.

Explain things to us so that we don't get curious and find out in other ways.[5]

The way in which we as parents relate to God depends on many factors in our own physical, emotional, moral, and spiritual development. If this is hindering us in our relationship with our teenagers, then we need to draw upon the resources the Lord provides in even greater measure. His love can blot out painful memories from the past, and His peace and presence can be our portion for now and the future. Think on these words which Jesus spoke to His disciples shortly before His betrayal and crucifixion. Let them burn into your thinking so that you can draw upon them at any time:

> I am the vine; you are the branches. If a man remains in me and I in him, he will bear much fruit; apart from me you can do nothing (John 15:5).

NOTES

1. Wilson, p. 55.
2. Ibid., pp. 64-65.
3. Shelly, p. 64.
4. Swindoll, p. 106.
5. Shelly, p. 72.

6

Being a Communicative Parent

When I was a boy in my father's house, still tender, and an only child of my mother, he taught me and said, "Lay hold of my words with all your heart; keep my commands and you will live."

Proverbs 4:3,4

If there is one statement I hear often from adolescents, it is, "I can't talk to my mom and dad. They're always so busy. And when they do take time to listen to me, I don't think they really hear what I'm saying." Words to that effect come across with more frequency than any other complaint that teenagers have about their parents. I think it's time we stop and listen—really listen—and make sure we are hearing—really hearing—what is being said. What is involved in being a communicative parent, one who is vitally interested in the welfare and words of his adolescent? Communication involves more than speaking. Let's begin by asking and answering the question, "What is communication?"

Communication: What It Is

Communication: 1. a transmitting. 2. a giving, or giving and receiving, of information, signals, or messages by talk, gestures, writing, etc.
Communicative: 1. giving information readily; talkative. 2. of communication.*

If communication is a transmitting, and a giving or a giving and receiving, of information, then why are adolescents saying their parents are

* *Webster's New World Dictionary, College Edition*

noncommunicative? No communication equals no relationship. Ruptured relationships are at the heart of parent-teen communication problems. Parents who bark out orders like a commanding officer and expect those orders to be heeded when there is not a good relationship with their teenager are barking up the wrong tree. Relationship always proceeds rules. I have talked to many young people who indicate in one way or another that they feel their parents only tolerate them. "They can't wait for me to leave home," is a common theme. I find this distressingly sad.

These parents probably were good parents for their babies, and they may even have done a good job in their children's early school years, but while their children were growing, changing, and maturing, the parents weren't! That may come as a rather startling statement to some readers, but there does come a point in time when we as parents must recognize that our parenting and communicating with our adolescents will need to take into consideration that their needs are not the same as they once were. Now they are starting to think for themselves. (Some of them are downright good thinkers, and parents should be thankful for that.) They are making new friends and are being exposed to a variety of different ideas.

A real problem that parents are facing is that they really don't have a message to give their teenager. I'm talking about a message that incorporates life principles. What does your *life*—not your words—say to your kids? Your actions, the things you do—are they consistent? Do they match up to what you are expecting from your adolescent?

One discerning mother observed several young parents in a restaurant smoking with babies in their laps and/or in high chairs. They were being rude to the waitress and generally quite disrespectful of other people around them. "I'll bet someday they yell at their kids and tell them not to smoke, not to drink, not to be impolite, etc.," she stated. The stage for noncommunication was being set early.

Moses, the spiritual leader of the Israelites, linked spiritual affirmations about God with family life.[1] Being communicative parents has a great deal to do with life principles being incorporated into one's walk as well as one's talk. Hear the wise counsel of Moses:

> Hear, O Israel: The Lord our God, the Lord is one. Love

the Lord your God with all your heart and with all your
soul and with all your strength. These commandments that
I give you today are to be upon your hearts. Impress them
on your children. Talk about them when you sit at home
and when you walk along the road, when you lie down
and when you get up. Tie them as symbols on your hands
and bind them on your foreheads. Write them on the door-
frames of your houses and on your gates (Deuteronomy
6:4-9).

That's a 24-hour-a-day responsibility. How do you measure up? That
wasn't just for Moses' day. Moses is telling us as parents that the central theme to our lives must revolve around the plan and presence of
God. It's a teach-and-talk routine. So often parents tell their kids what
they expect but never bother to explain why: "Just do it because I
say so." They won't listen to their teenager's questions, suggestions,
or comments. Life at home is living under a dictatorship—if it's not
dad, it's mom, and oftentimes it's both parents screaming out orders
with no consideration of the child himself.

Is it any wonder that teenagers of today seek escape in other-world
reality through tripping out on drugs or sexual encounters? They are
hungry for attention, love, acceptance, and understanding. Parents are
starving their teenagers emotionally, not attempting to understand
adolescents' underlying problems so they can help them with their struggles. Dr. Bruce Narramore (psychologist plus marriage, family, and child
counselor in California) states that rules and regulations are a cheap
substitute for understanding and are often imposed as a last-ditch
effort when parents feel that all else has failed. What does this do?
It only stirs up more resentment.

Communication involves taking time to understand, and that comes
through listening sympathetically with a hearing heart. It doesn't mean
that parents don't have rules or that they abandon guidelines. It *does*
mean that we respect our teenagers' need to express their point of
view and that we attempt to understand where they are coming from—
their perspective. There are ways to take the sting out of parental pro-
hibitions. Dr. Narramore warns against extremes—being too permissive
or too restrictive. The areas about which teens come into conflict with

their parents at an early age usually revolve around social activities (dating), driving (use of the car), and wanting to be their own boss. They need parental guidance and controls because the opportunities and responsibilities out there in the world are frightening and overwhelming.

Involve your teenagers in your decision-making. Ask them what they think is a reasonable hour to be in. Ask them to share with you some information about their friends and the types of activities they intend to participate in. Let them know what they can look forward to, but also what the limitations are and that violations may impose some serious restrictions next time. This ought to develop a sense of security and recognition that you are genuinely concerned, that you are communicating, and that you are going to trust them. Give them freedom gradually; be gracious without being permissive to an extreme.

Here are some guidelines to help you choose the limits you will set for your teenagers—limits that will help to cultivate communication. They have been compiled by Dr. Narramore.[2]

1. *Recognize that every person is different.*

If there's one thing that turns teens off it's to have their parents or other adults constantly say to them, "When I was your age...." What was right for you as a teenager, or what is right for someone else's teenager, is not necessarily suitable for your adolescent.

2. *Discuss the possible limits with your teenager before making a decision.*

Try to have an open mind; don't be so defensive that your teenager will (rightly) accuse you of not listening and of being noncommunicative.

3. *Differentiate between a Biblical absolute and your personal preference.*

I've had teenagers tell me their parents insisted that something was Biblical and that's why they were demanding conformity from them. You had better be certain that the Bible clearly supports your position or the kids will say we've been putting words in God's mouth. Parents get in lots of arguments with their teenagers about hair length, certain styles of dress, and whether they can or cannot go to movies or dance, etc. If you are convinced, then take the time to explain the "why" to your son or daughter, and back it up by showing him or her from the Bible.

4. *Be flexible.*

Dr. Narramore points out that there are usually reasonable exceptions to most rules, and that a special situation with proper safeguards may call for revised limits.

5. *Compare your standards to those of a variety of other parents.*

Parents are accused of being narrow-minded. By comparing your standards with those of other parents in a reasonable way and communicating your own values and beliefs, you should be able to set limits that other parents don't have, and your teenager should be able to see that this is good and has his best interests at heart.

6. *Work toward cooperative development of standards.*

Narramore warns of getting in the position where you are acting and looking like a policeman or judge. Instead, remember that you want to communicate to your teenager that you are a loving, caring parent.

7. *Allow increasing freedom and responsibility with increasing age.*

You can explain to your 16-year-old, "You are in a better position now to make wise decisions than you were two years ago; and by the time you're in your late teens, you will be even more capable." This will encourage responsible decision-making. You aren't *taking away* freedoms; you're *giving* freedoms according to the wisdom that their age indicates. Remember, communication is giving and receiving, and you can remind them that it's a two-way street.

8. *Never set a limit without giving a good reason.*

That only makes good sense. A friend relates that her two-year-old granddaughter is very good already at asking "Why?" and she wonders what she'll be like when she's a teenager. She expects and requires answers even at two. But if parents will make that effort to communicate answers all along the line, the teenager should understand that the parent isn't merely trying to control him but is trying to help him avoid painful experiences and to make good choices throughout life.

These things should improve parent-teen communication.

Unfreezing Communication Channels

Everything I read points to the need for family members to be friends as well as parents, brothers, sisters, etc.

How do you relate to your friends? Do you accuse them of never listening to you and of being out of touch? Of course not! Then don't do that to your teenagers. While teenagers accuse parents of not listening, parents do the same thing. That's wrong. That's not working to build a relationship. This kind of name-calling and accusation freezes communication channels. Since this book is addressed to parents, I must focus on trying to help you see that resorting to angry outbursts is not going to accomplish what you wish. (But I want you to know that in my assemblies and in conversations with your teenagers I get the message across to them also.)

Respect the other person enough to hear him out. The Lord of the universe is listening, and what He hears must often grieve His heart. The Bible has a lot to say about controlling one's tongue (see Job 19:2; James 3:7-10; Proverbs 15:23). Words have the power to heal or harm. Communication foul-ups can be avoided by stopping for a moment or two to reflect on what you are about to say. You've heard of the pause that refreshes? Try it—I think you'll like it and the difference it can make in your relationship with your adolescent.

Jesus called His disciples friends (see John 15:15). Friends have fellowship with each other. In this too we have the example of Jesus. Can we be like Jesus in our parenting skills? I believe we can, and this involves saying to our children, "Let's be friends." I'm thrilled when I hear parents and teenagers say of each other, "My dad is my best friend," or a mother will say, "My daughter and I are the dearest of friends now." This is possible and desirable.

In my research I have discovered that almost every writer on parenting relationships urges that parents cultivate this kind of friendship relationship. This is something that should be developing naturally through their formative years—when we play ball with them, shop together, go camping, etc. If we've given of ourselves in this way, it is almost certain that by the time they reach adolescence they will want us involved in their lives as friends and close confidants. They have learned to see us as people who know how to laugh and cry with them. It is possible for parents to genuinely enjoy their teenagers, and I feel sorry for moms and dads who do not have this kind of relationship. But it's never too late to work to acquire it. Remember, never give up on your teenagers. (And don't give up on yourself either.)

By being friends with them we can help them make the transition from childhood into young adulthood, and then we more readily gain a platform for giving counsel and direction. It really does work that way. Narramore says that in essence we earn the right to lead, counsel, and discipline our teenagers by being their friends as well as their parents. We build an affectionate bond that makes them want to listen and to value what we say. And we reduce the potential friction and resentment when we do set limits on their actions.[3]

Dr. Narramore issues a word of caution which is well-taken. By being friends with our children we shouldn't give them the impression that we are abdicating our parental responsibilities or attempting to be "one of the gang." They want us to be able to relate to them and their friends without being too buddy-buddy. How do we do this? We share their interests, we spend time with them, we open them up to new insights on life, we take an active interest in their activities, and we offer help when it's appropriate and we can provide it. But, on the other hand, we don't intrude.

Communication Skills to Develop

Many excellent resource materials are available which I urge parents to read, study, and apply in their attempts to improve communication levels with family members. In addition to the authors whom I have quoted and referred to (see footnotes section following each chapter), I have been especially blessed in my own reading by Norman Wright and Rex Johnson's book *Communication: Key to Your Teens*. One of the things they say is that so many parents fear adolescence because they equate changing relationships with alienation. They expect rebellion, maybe embarrassment, a fracturing of family relationships, and deep hurts.

But these two authors emphasize that it doesn't have to be this way. "Just because relationships change doesn't mean they have to get worse.'' They show that good communication and conflict-resolution patterns can reduce the severity of most of the problems that parents face with their teenagers.

Don Highlander, a licensed marriage and family therapist, has some highly motivating things to say in his book *Positive Parenting*. In speaking of communication, he shows how it is a learning process and that there are several important communication skills which parents can strive for:

1. To learn to listen to what other people say and feel.
2. To learn to clarify incoming messages, to see beyond the words to what is actually being expressed.
3. To focus on the person when listening and the problem when responding.
4. To understand and show concern in a way that lets the other person know that his feelings are important, and that our empathy is genuine.
5. To clearly communicate our feelings to other people by accurate feedback.[4]

He goes on to explain that when a person speaks, there are actually eight facets to the message:

1. What the person is *thinking and feeling*.
2. What he *means* to say.
3. What he *actually* says.
4. What he does *nonverbally* that influences the meaning of what he's trying to say.
5. What the listener *hears or thinks he hears*.
6. What the listener *interprets* from the verbal and nonverbal message.
7. What the listener *adds* to the message because of his own feelings, experiences, or perceptions.
8. What the listener says in *response*.[5]

So communication is more than talking, it's also listening. And a good listener, taking all of the above facets into consideration. ''For parents, effective listening focuses on the child, rather than on any problem at hand....Listening is not passive; it is an active process of reaching out and caring—responding, clarifying, and expressing acceptance and understanding."[6]

Listening is another way of loving our children. It should be our desire to put to silence those complaints of adolescents who cry out, "My parents don't really hear what I'm saying when I try to talk to them."

Why Do Our Children Cut Off Communication?

Not all communication problems are the parents' fault. Let me assure you that I am quick to point this out to teenagers. Here are a few of the reasons why our children sever the communication lines.

1. Our response as parents is too predictable. This is closely related to being a poor listener. Our teenagers have come to expect that we will tune them out. Parents have an annoying habit of answering their children before the poor kid even asks the question. "No, you can't go out tonight." "What do you mean, Dad? I wasn't going to ask to go out tonight." "Well, you can't go out tomorrow night either." "I didn't intend to—" "Nor this weekend."

Do you recall any conversations similar to that one?

However, having pointed out that fault to you, I hasten to remind your teenagers that sometimes they invite predictable answers by *their* approach.

This leads to a second reason why communication suffers.

2. There is personal guilt about wrong actions. The teenagers are struggling with sin in their lives. (See 1 Samuel 15 and note the progression of sin—it began with a lie and deception, moved on to arrogance as a cover-up, and then resulted in rejection of the Word of the Lord. See also Colossians 3:5, which portrays the struggle with sexual sin and its downward path.)

When you sin there's guilt. (See Ephesians 6. Disobedience to parents and to what our teenagers know the Bible says brings with it a subsequent disquieting "reward"—guilt.)

Your adolescent will cut off communication because of sin and the resulting guilt. Teenagers think its easier to shun their parents than to face up to their wrongdoing. Remember the little child's actions when he's done something wrong? He squeezes his eyes shut real tight. Now he can't see the spilled milk and he wants to think that his mother can't see it either.

3. A third reason why adolescents refuse to communicate is because they hate to let you down. Why? Because they fear punishment. Why do they hate punishment? Because punishment is a restraint.

Society has jammed down our throats the idea that everyone has the right to freedom. Much has been said in recent years about children's rights. Our kids have swallowed that line without thinking through its many ramifications. The message coming through to them is "I'm free to do as I please. I don't have to listen to anybody, especially my folks." But in their more serious, reflective moments, they realize that by letting you down they've rightfully incurred your mistrust. They really are anxious about being mistrusted. How many times have your teenagers said to you "What's wrong? Don't you trust me?" They do want to be trusted.

They also recognize that by letting you down both you and they are going to be hurt. When you love someone deeply, you don't want to hurt him.

Even if they come off as being caustic, they aren't uncaring. They may camouflage their feelings, but at just such a time they need you to reach out to them, put your arms around them, and reassure them that even though they've disappointed you, it hasn't changed your love for them.

You Can Be a Communicative Parent

The way in which you communicate with God and the way in which He communicates with you forms the pattern for you to follow in your relationships with your adolescent. When you accepted God's forgiveness, you walked into outstretched arms of love. You then learned to communicate with God through prayer and by spending time in His written Word to you. You worshiped Him in fellowship with other believers in church and in Bible studies. Think about these things and move on and out into a deeper level of communicating with your family through sharing, caring, and responding. Let your teenager know that he is loved, trusted, understood, and cared for. Let him know that fellowship with him makes you happy and joyful. Let him know that you always want to keep those communication channels open, responsive, and receptive.

NOTES

1. MacDonald, *The Effective Father,* p. 45.
2. Bruce Narramore, *Adolescence Is Not an Illness* (Old Tappan, New Jersey: Fleming H. Revell Co., 1980), pp. 67-68.
3. Ibid., p. 77.
4. Don H. Highlander, *Positive Parenting* (Waco, Texas: Word Books, 1980), pp. 83-84.
5. Ibid., p. 87.
6. Ibid., p. 88.

7

The Sexual Revolution: The "Wrongs" About Children's "Rights"

For a man's ways are in full view of the Lord, and he examines all his paths.

Proverbs 5:21

Parents of this generation are confronted with a harsh reality: things have changed since you were a teenager. Sometimes parents get the feeling that they are in the midst of a trackless wilderness. The traditional American family is under attack. Frustrated parents are angry, hurt, and bewildered. One disturbed parent said, "It takes a lot of courage to raise kids today."

And it's nationwide. These demoralized, alienated, and troubled parents can be found in one community after another—big cities, small towns, middle-class suburbia, country folk—and among the rich as well as the poor. No one is unaffected, it seems, by this sexually permissive society. The tragedy is that our sons and daughters are the ones most directly affected.

Not only is there a nationwide financial bill staring taxpayers in the face yearly as a result of sexual promiscuity, but there are the hidden costs. The greater cost is what this is doing to young people unprepared for the harsh realities of out-of-wedlock adolescent pregnancies, or the later trauma that will come as a result of an abortion. And what are we to say about the price of the broken hearts of moms and dads?

The figures reveal that 50 percent of the nation's 10.3 million teenage women (15-19 years) have had premarital sex. That figure has increased 100 percent since 1971! One million teenage girls will become pregnant this year. Six hundred thousand of those teens will give birth, with the sharpest increase coming to girls 14 years of age and under—children giving birth to children.

One out of five girls, before she reaches the age of 13, will have sexual intercourse. This is moral chaos. We've had more than a generation of sexual show-and-tell in our public schools, and we've been deluged with sex in one form or another on television and in the printed media. Television glamorizes infidelity. The subtle innuendos on talk shows and accompanying snickers from the participants, the hosts, and the audience have not gone unnoticed by young, impressionable minds. Off-color humor jumps out at the viewer, and marital infidelity is mocked or openly ridiculed. Pick up a magazine and you are launched on a pornographic trip—almost any magazine.

The Fort Worth Star-Telegram (July 15, 1982) hits the reader in the face with the headline, "No End To Herpes In Sight."

> Don't hold your breath for herpes to vanish. The virus has no cure, and only cursory treatments. It remains a mystery disease for which authorities can only guess how many people are infected. Unlike syphilis and gonorrhea, law does not require doctors to report instances of herpes to the government....
>
> Without hard statistics, authorities estimate that 20-50 million Americans have herpes. It is believed to be primarily a white, middle- to upper-class phenomenon, rampant on...campuses and in young adults....Of the sexually transmitted diseases, only gonorrhea is more widespread.

These sexually transmitted diseases are equal-opportunity diseases—boys as well as girls, men as well as women, contract them. These diseases are impacting the health of our children and their future offspring. These diseases can cause serious birth defects, including blindness. Those who insist that our children need sex education in public classrooms point to such facts when trying to convince school boards and parents that sex ed courses are the answer. And in state after state, such courses have been adopted. The cry has gone out that parents aren't doing their job in properly informing their kids, so it's up to the school to take over this responsibility. The result? Amoral teaching stripped of anything that reflects traditional parental sexual standards and beliefs; the handing out of contraceptives in classrooms; the easy availability of abortion as a backup to unwanted pregnancy without parental consent; the acceptance of homosexuality as an alternate lifestyle; the encouragement of masturbation; an advocating of adult rights for children; the use of materials that can only be described as graphically pornographic in content; and a failure to teach the dangers of early sexual activity and cervical cancer, with a general screening and evasion of the subject of venereal disease.

I have only skimmed the surface of what has been happening in this sexual revolution that considers marriage dispensable and sexual restraint by young people to be a type of Victorian repression. One professional writer of articles on family and marital relations and education polled mothers and fathers of 402 families across the country to obtain their opinions and personal experiences. She asked them to talk about their grievances and what was distressing them the most as they saw the fabric of the American family being torn apart. As they zeroed in on the "wrongs" about children's rights, Jeane Westin compiled some interesting facts and statistics.

> Of the parents interviewed, 93 percent thought their children's sexual awareness was running well ahead of their ability to cope with the consequences of sexual behavior.

> Sixty-three percent of the parents taught their children that premarital sex and living together were wrong.

> Ninety-eight percent of the parents thought extramarital sex was wrong and passed that belief on to their children.

> Few of these parents felt relaxed about their children's sex lives.

> Ninety-six percent of the parents said they gave their children verbal sexual instruction, either in the form of answering questions or of acceptable literature.

> Fifty-six percent of the parents said they gave specific contraceptive information.

> Eighty-nine percent reported using these occasions of talking about sex to impart moral training, but only about half of these believed that their children benefited. The other half believed that their children thought they were out of date.

Almost all of these parents emphatically disagreed with the idea that their children have any right to sexual activity. (This is contrary to the teachings of sex educators, whose battle cry is, "What one does with one's own body is the business of only the person involved.")

The parental consensus, even among self-styled 1960s rebels now entering their thirties, is that "sex is not children's entertainment" and "the glandular whims of adolescents don't ...assume the consequences of the sex act." Few parents saw teenagers as capable of accepting this responsibility.

All of these parents expressed concern over how far sex instruction has strayed from the biology of human development—the kind of sexual instruction in the schools that most parents support—and has marched in the direction of self-awareness and acceptance of one's own sexuality.[1]

Parents have had to carry the brunt of the blame from those interested in promoting their sexual conglomerate—the public-health and social-health establishment, the psychosexual movement, and such organizations as Planned Parenthood and SIECUS (the Sex Information and Education Council of the United States). We're talking about big bucks—something like 200 million dollars in federal Title X subsidy programs!

The rationale behind school sex ed programs has been that adequate information would lead to responsible behavior. Have these programs accomplished their goals? Financed with taxpayer's money, this "advanced," "discover yourself" sex education has failed miserably. *Newsweek* reported that an estimated 80 percent of sexually active teenagers fail to use birth control. Meanwhile, abortion figures throughout the nation continue to climb, with more than a million-and-a-half babies being killed annually (compared to the 1970 figure of 190,000). I have already reported the facts about what this is doing to the health of our young people.

With this information as background, I want to give you some ideas on how you can handle sex talks with your sons and daughters. I have been helped in my research by the book *The Parent's Guide To Teen-*

Age Sex and Pregnancy, by Howard and Martha Lewis. As concerned Christian parents we must face the fact that this sexual revolution is upon us and that we can't shield our children. We must arm them and must come to grips with the Scriptural teachings about sexuality ourselves. We must then perpetuate these truths, handing them down to be preserved from one generation to another within our families.

How to Handle Sex Talks

1. *Start early.* No matter how old their children are, when people ask me, "When do I begin to counsel my children about sex?" I have a one-word, short answer—NOW.

If your children are very young, you might consider using the book *You and Me and Our New Little Baby.*[2] Maxine Hancock has some excellent suggestions in her book *Confident Creative Children*[3] (in the chapter titled "Body Truth").

Parents need to be frank but not too explicit in fitting the information they impart to their children's present sexual knowledge. Other books for use with smaller children include *Susie's Babies*[4] and *I Wonder, I Wonder.*[5] Grace Ketterman, M.D., has written a thoroughly Scriptural, practical approach to sex education entitled *How To Teach Your Child About Sex.*[6]

But begin now, because I can promise you that your children already know something about sex. Of course, if they are teenagers they definitely have been talking about it and thinking about it.

2. *Take the initiative.* It's embarrassing to your teenager to ask you questions about sexual matters. It's far wiser for you to take the initiative by seizing "teachable moments"—occasions when your child is likely to be the most receptive to sexual information or guidance. The Lewises suggest that you watch physical changes in your child—when pubic hair sprouts, breasts bud, menstruation occurs, or there is a growth spurt. These are perfect occasions to expand your child's sexual knowledge. You can also watch for teachable moments in television programs or in newspaper or magazine articles.

3. *Keep it casual.* This isn't the time for dad to dress up in his suit, vest, and tie, profusely sweating, as he contemplates taking his son

aside for a good "man-to-man" talk. No lectures!

Take your son fishing; or you, mother, take your daughter out for a special lunch. Spontaneous exchanges are best; your child will feel relaxed and comfortable when you don't force the issue. You don't have to cover the whole subject of sex in one sitting, either. Leave the door open for more discussions in the future. Assure your child that sex is a God-given gift, and that it's nothing to be embarrassed or ashamed of, and that you want him/her to feel at ease with you about any aspects of the subject.

4. *Help your child to trust you.* Let your child know that you understand his/her sexual drives. Your son and/or daughter needs help and ideas on how to control his/her thoughts. Help him/her to understand how they can relate to the opposite sex without feelings of guilt. Boys will be attracted to girls; girls will be attracted to boys. This is natural. Show the child that overcoming temptation is a way of life, that this is the old battle of the flesh, but that through relying on the strength God supplies, we can always be equal to any temptation. When your child sees that you are saying it's okay to be human, he/she will be much more likely to trust you and to confide in you in the future.

5. *Answer the questions that are asked.* We should be the source of our children's information. So be ready to answer your child's questions at face value. Reply factually and resist jumping to conclusions. Example: if your daughter wants to know, "Are birth-control pills really dangerous?" don't assume she's asking because she wants to take them.

The Lewises tell of a young girl, Erika, whose friend Mindy had missed her period. Both girls were virgins. So Erika asked her mother, "How can a person tell if she's pregnant?" How do you suppose Erika's mother answered? Without stopping to think, she jumped on her daughter, "Are you pregnant?" That kind of response is going to turn a daughter away from her mother, and she'll cease coming to her for advice. Don't pounce on your teenager when he/she comes with questions, and don't be suspicious of him/her. If you do have some fears, probe with caution. Ask the Lord to give you His supernatural wisdom. Fear of embarrassment or disapproval has kept many a young person from seeking out the kind of information he needs from his parents. Assure your son or daughter that he or she doesn't ever have to feel embarrassed to ask questions of you.

6. *Yield if you meet resistance.* "Oh, I already know all that stuff," your teenager may say when you bring up the subject. Don't get frustrated by that kind of response. That's a defensive tactic used because the kid is sort of embarrassed. Most 13-year-olds have that "know-it-all" attitude on most subjects anyway, so what's so unusual about that kind of response? Don't be pushy or get upset. Just reply, "Okay, we'll talk about it some other time." You might even add, "Let me know when you want to ask some questions."

Respect your child's need for privacy. He just doesn't want to be put on the spot, so don't come on as being intrusive. Prying parents can unintentionally help their children to build up a wall of noncommunication. That's what you want to avoid. So be a praying parent instead and ask the Lord to give you the right time with your child so that proper information can be imparted.

7. *Use the proper terms.* Don't back off from using precise medical terminology. You don't want to talk down to your children, and this is an excellent way to make certain you're not doing that. Technical terms are less emotionally charged than some of the slang words or euphemisms which have been developed for describing genitalia or sexual activities. Some of those terms are downright vulgar and are most inappropriate. The following words convey clear meanings: penis, vagina, hymen, clitoris, menstruation, orgasm, breasts, erection, masturbation, condoms, testicles, semen, ejaculation. You don't want this subject to be made mysterious and obscure to your teenagers, because the more mysterious it is, the more they're going to delve into it secretly and perhaps destructively.

8. *Give an accurate picture.* Bill Mauldin in the *Washington Post* had a terrific cartoon of a kid coming home from school, throwing open the door, and standing there shouting: "Okay! Everyone in this house please stand advised that I, Thomas P. Thompson, have this date made a complete fool of myself in sex-education class by relating elaborate stories concerning storks told to me by certain parties residing herein!"

We can laugh at that, but the point is to avoid repeating myths or trying to "protect" your child from sexual truths, because you will only risk discrediting yourself and losing face with your son or daughter in the long run. Be truthful, and don't be evasive. Relate the facts and be accurate.

Some parents are just naturally inhibited and can't bring themselves to tackle the subject of explaining sex to their children. If that's your situation, then face up to it. Do try, however, to provide your son or daughter with reliable reading material that can help him or her. You might investigate whether there is someone in your church who would consider having a class for teenagers. But don't neglect your parental responsibility; your child needs some confidant, instructor, and/or adviser. Perhaps you will want to make an appointment with your doctor to have him explain these facts of life to your child. There may be a nurse friend or someone competent in your circle of friends to whom you could turn.

9. *Tell your children about your moral convictions.* It's one thing to be sexually knowledgeable, but it's another thing to be sexually responsible. There are no in-between standards when it comes to sex. The only acceptable standard for the Christian is a clear-cut adherence to the Biblical standard. Sex outside of marriage is forbidden. This is not what kids are getting in most sex ed classes today, nor from the non-Christian books and secular reading materials on the newsstands and general bookstores.

You as a parent not only have the right to declare to your children what your moral convictions are, but it is your responsibility under God to do this. Husbands and wives need to set aside time to discuss this between themselves, and then they need to be able to back up each moral value they wish to convey to their children with Biblical support. If you don't, your standards won't make any difference to your teens. They've heard in school and from classmates, as well as from the media, that they should be free to form their own values without adult and parental interference.

Perhaps you're thinking, "How do I go about this? How do I present these Biblical standards to my children?" To make it easy for you, I'm setting these standards down and backing them up with the appropriate Bible reference.

Sexual temptation   Genesis 39

This is the account of Joseph fleeing temptation when Potiphar's wife tried repeatedly to lure him to go to bed with her. Notice Joseph's reply to her, and emphasize this to your children: "How then could I do such a wicked thing and sin against God?" (verse 9).

Getting involved with the wrong fellow or girl   Judges 16

Samson's affinity for the wrong women—in particular, Delilah—cost him his great strength, his physical sight, and finally his life.

The consequences of sinful sexual indulgence   2 Samuel 11,12

Passion overruled better judgment, and David committed adultery with Bath-sheba. The Bible is faithful in its condemnation of sin, even sins of a David. "But the thing David had done displeased the Lord" (2 Samuel 11:27).

God has a perfect plan for our lives   Genesis 24

In the story of Isaac and Rebekah we see how God's plan for putting a young man and a young woman together unfolds. In God's perfect timing, if it is His will that our children marry, then He can be counted upon to bring that right person into their lives.

The folly of sexual sin   The Book of Proverbs

Proverbs is loaded with wisdom describing the folly of sexual sin. The moral benefits that accrue to the person who heeds these instructions are great. Chapters 5, 6, and 7 contain special words of insight regarding the sin of adultery. "The corrections of discipline are the way of life, keeping you from the immoral woman.... Do not lust in your heart after her beauty or let her captivate you with her eyes, for the prostitute reduces you to a loaf of bread, and the adulteress preys upon your very life. Can a man scoop fire into his lap without his clothes being burned? Can a man walk on hot coals without his feet being scorched?" (Proverbs 6:23-28).

The pleasure of sexual love in marriage   The Song of Solomon

This is a beautiful representation of pure human love. Its subject is the deepest emotion of the soul.

Rules for holy living; God's hatred   Colossians 3:1-17;
of sexual immorality   Revelation 21:6-8

God's disgust for unlawful sexual intercourse (fornication) is clearly stated. "Because of these, the wrath of God is coming" (Colossians 3:6).

Premarriage and marriage relationships   1 Corinthians 7

These are very important teachings. "Keeping God's commands is what counts" (1 Corinthians 7:19) is what Paul emphasizes.

Sex Is God's Idea

What am I trying to say? What should our children understand about sex? Simply this: sex is God's idea. You and I didn't think it up. God is very interested in the whole process—conception, birth, the cradle, early, mid- and later childhood, adolescence, and our more-mature years. At every stage we are sexual beings. You are the one who must talk to them about such things as masturbation, oral sex, petting, and intercourse.

We tell our children, "...male and female he created them" (Genesis 1:27). Our sexuality is an essential part of our divinely created nature. Because sex comes from God, it is basically good. It becomes defiled when we misuse or abuse our bodies or someone else's body. That's why God places sexual intercourse within the bounds of marriage—so that two people who truly love each other will treat the other person's body with respect. God has a purpose behind the sexual act. Yes, it is pleasurable, but it is also for procreation, to perpetuate the human race. We are therefore to act as responsible stewards with this gift as with all the gifts He gives to us.

Our children also need to learn that the Bible condemns such sexual abuses as homosexuality and bestiality. In the Old Testament book of Leviticus the homosexual act is called an abomination which is detestable to the Lord (Leviticus 20:13). That same passage says, "If a man has sexual relations with an animal, he must be put to death, and you must kill the animal" (verse 15). God does not wink at sin.

> Do you not know that the wicked will not inherit the kingdom of God? Do not be deceived: Neither the sexually immoral nor idolaters nor adulterers nor male prostitutes nor homosexual offenders nor theives nor the greedy nor drunkards nor slanderers nor swindlers will inherit the

kingdom of God. And that is what some of you were. But
you were washed, you were sanctified, you were justified
in the name of the Lord Jesus Christ and by the Spirit of
our God (1 Corinthians 6:9-11).

These verses show God's abhorrence for sexual sin; they also
demonstrate that abnormal sexual appetites can be brought under the
power and control of the Holy Spirit.

Putting Sex in Perspective

We are to honor God with our bodies. There are some things that
are more important for your children to realize than just the mechanics
of sex and how the sexual organs function. Granted, that's what the
kids are interested in and that's one of the reasons they experiment.
But that's why I believe that as parents it's so important for us to help
our children get sex in perspective. First, let's look at some more strong
words from the Apostle Paul in this regard:

"Everything is permissible for me"—but not everything
is beneficial. "Everything is permissible for me"—but I
will not be mastered by anything. "Food for the stomach
and the stomach for food"—but God will destroy them
both. The body is not meant for sexual immorality, but
for the Lord, and the Lord for the body. By His power God
raised the Lord from the dead, and He will raise us also.
Do you not know that your bodies are members of Christ
himself? Shall I then take the members of Christ and unite
them with a prostitute? Never! Do you not know that he
who unites himself with a prostitute is one with her in
body? For it is said, "The two will become one flesh."
But he who unites himself with the Lord is one with Him
in spirit.

Flee from sexual immorality. All other sins a man commits
are outside his body, but he who sins sexually sins against
his own body. Do you not know that your body is a
temple of the Holy Spirit, who is in you, whom you have
received from God? You are not your own; you were bought

at a price. Therefore honor God with your body (1 Corinthians 6:12-20).

What are the important issues that surround the mechanics of the sexual experience?

Patience: Our children must be taught and shown that patience is all-important. To everything there is a season, a right time, and sexual experimentation before marriage is not included in God's timetable. Some of our Christian young people act as though they think Christ is going to come back before they even have a chance to get married and have sex. Well, praise the Lord if that were to happen, but try and convince the kids! We can make light of that, but it's serious business. They must be convinced.

Let me tell you something—the kids are not half as excited about getting married as they are about having sex.

Our children need to be told that God knows and understands their desires. But when the Bible says, "Wait on the Lord," it means just that. That word in its Hebrew text means to delay with silent anticipation. Have you ever anticipated something bad? No, when you hear the word "anticipation," right away you think about good things. You anticipate a pay raise; you anticipate the upcoming holiday, the vacation the family's getting ready to take. You anticipate buying a new car. You never anticipate a headache or "I think I'm going to get killed in a car accident this week." You don't anticipate that sort of thing. Anticipation connotes enjoyable excitement.

When the Lord says to wait, He is talking about excitement—to delay in silent excitement for what is to come. That's what being patient in this area of sex is all about.

Let us help our young people to realize that sex is a beautiful gift, something that is intrinsically good. God made our sexual impulses and desires. When He looked upon Adam and Eve, He could say that what He had made was very good (Genesis 1:31). God intends for it to remain that way, and our children should be made to realize that if they will wait patiently, God in His perfect time will bless them with exactly the right mate.

Full-time commitment: Let us teach our children that marriage is to be a full-time commitment to the same person. Never has the challenge set before parents been greater. With the divorce rate at an all-time high and going higher each year, we must not fail in this God-given responsibility.

God is not for divorce. This doesn't mean that God will not forgive divorced individuals, but it means that *God is not for it*; He does not like it. God hates divorce (Malachi 2:16). Marriage is a full-time commitment. You may be a divorced individual, or a divorced and remarried couple, or divorce may have hit other family members (aunts, uncles, parents—your children's grandparents, your children's brothers or sisters), but that doesn't excuse anyone. In their relationships, our children need to hear from us that marriage is for keeps.

If kids would fully fathom that, I'm convinced that they wouldn't be nearly as anxious about sex. We must emphasize commitment— the fact that sex is more than a feeling. We as youth counselors often hear, "Well, I believe it's not wrong or it's not a sin to have sex if you really love the person." That's a timeworn cop-out if ever I heard one. We have an answer: "Well, if you really love a person and are committed to him, you will never do anything that would hinder him or rip him off in any way. This means that you will not steal his virtue from him, because you are committed to him. A person isn't just a piece of flesh that we use and get rid of after we've finished with him. Each person is a human being with an eternal soul for whom Christ died. If we're going to invade the flesh of a person, it had better be with a full-time commitment within the bonds of marriage."

I tell kids about my own experience in my relationship with my wife, Robyn, prior to our marriage. I was a typical teenage guy—ready to tell a girl I loved her on the first date. But six months before I met Robyn the Lord began dealing with me. I made a commitment to Him that I would never again tell a woman I loved her unless I was ready in the same breath to ask her to marry me. So when I met Robyn— who was really that someone special, and I knew it—I felt the strongest urge to say, "Robyn, I love you." But even though I knew she was someone special, it still wasn't love. Love takes time. You have to get to know someone. *It was total infatuation.* There is a difference. Now total infatuation can grow quickly into love, but then again it can sour too. In our case, it grew into love.

Robyn and I had a long-distance love relationship. She was living in Missouri and I was living in Minneapolis, and we were commuting back and forth about every six weeks or so to see each other. After about four months of this I decided that I was going to tell her that I loved her. I'll never forget the night. It was in the living room of my parents' home. I had my arm around her and I said, "Look that way," and I pointed in the opposite direction. My heart was pounding to beat the band. I was shaking and sweat was pouring off my head. She turned her head and looked, and then I whispered, "I love you." Three months after that I was able to think in terms of marriage, and I knew it was God's timing.

Don't harbor unnecessary guilt feelings: It's important for Christian young people to recognize that they don't have to feel guilty over having sexual thoughts. All of us, from time to time, have passing sexual thoughts and fantasies. But for the young person these thoughts can get blown out of proportion. Then the teenagers become so bogged down with guilt that they can't even function. Parents notice something's wrong, but they can't figure out what. And the kid's sure not going to tell them. So, parents, allay those fears and help your kids to realize that it's perfectly normal to have passing sexual thoughts.

Then go a step further and explain that when they begin to dwell on those thoughts they run the risk of becoming immoral, because then they become heart thoughts. So often the heart thoughts get acted out; the kid succumbs to temptation and ends up in trouble. Give your children these verses so they can understand that what you are saying is taught by the Bible:

> My son, if your heart is wise,
>   then my heart will be glad;
> my inmost being will rejoice
>   when your lips speak what is right.
> Do not let your heart envy sinners,
>   but always be zealous for the fear of the Lord.
> There is surely a future hope for you,
>   and your hope will not be cut off.

Listen, my son, and be wise,
   and keep your heart on the right path....
My son, give me your heart
   and let your eyes keep to my ways.

Proverbs 23:15-19,26

...whatever is true, whatever is noble, whatever is right, whatever
is pure, whatever is lovely, whatever is admirable—if anything
is excellent or praiseworthy—think about such things.

Philippians 4:8

Our children need to be taught that thoughts can corrupt. The Apostle
Paul had some words and advice on how to win that kind of battle:

For though we walk in the flesh, we do not war after the flesh;
for the weapons of our warfare are not carnal [of the flesh], but
mighty through God to the pulling down of strongholds; casting
down imaginations, and every high thing that exalteth itself against
the knowledge of God, and bringing into captivity every thought
to the obedience of Christ.

2 Corinthians 10:3-5 (KJV)

Elsewhere he tells his readers that they need to examine and test
themselves to see whether they are really in the faith. There is a holy
fear that must be instilled into the hearts of young people. We should
tell them, "What are your motives? Would your secret thoughts bear
scrutiny? Remember, even though other people cannot read your mind
and heart, God can and does."

Jesus had something to say about our thought life.

"You have heard that it was said, 'Do not commit adultery.' But
I tell you that anyone who looks at a woman lustfully has already
committed adultery with her in his heart."

Matthew 5:27

Adultery is not just a physical act; it is defilement of the heart. Dr.
Lester Sumrall in his book *60 Things God Said About Sex* says, "You
are just as guilty of adultery as if you had paid for an overnight motel
room and taken the woman with you" if you harbor these lustful
thoughts in your heart. Teach your children to recognize lust for what
it really is—a sin against Almighty God!

How to Be Overcomers

We and our children can resist temptation in several ways. We can look to Jesus as our example. When He was tempted by Satan in the wilderness (see Matthew 4), Jesus turned his thoughts to Scripture. At the very moment that Satan started tempting Him, Jesus said, "It is written...." He did the same thing when the devil took Him to the highest point of the temple in Jerusalem, and when he led Him to a very high mountain. In each instance Jesus countered the devil's attack with Scripture.

Children should be taught to put their lives into the perspective of eternity. Impress upon them to think about the eternal consequences of their course of action. "Would Jesus approve of this?" "Will this keep me from heaven?" Sexual temptation can lose its allure when we get our focus right.

The third thing that can be done to help our children cope with their sexuality is to put limitations on their activities—to help them avoid situations in which they will be tempted. Of course we can't shield our children forever, but neither do we have to thrust them out into situations for which they are not yet prepared.

In Summary

By carefully undergirding our children's knowledge of sex with teaching in the home, we can trust God to help us achieve the end result—children who have a sane, balanced, healthy, and respectful attitude toward their own and other people's sexuality. We can then expect that our adolescents will accept and respect their own bodies as God's plan and design, and that they will always recognize that God has set forth rules meant for their own good, happiness, and fulfillment. We can believe and claim for our children that they will move on into maturity with sound character that manifests itself outwardly in self-respect, self-discipline, and a responsible attitude toward themselves and other people. We can help them achieve all of this with minds unclouded by guilt and with joyous anticipation of someday entering into a marriage relationship in which they and their children can be procreators with God.

Let us consistently remind our children that the beginning of purity in an impure world is the cleansing blood of Jesus, and that the continuation of it comes as we stay in the Word.

> Wherewithal shall a young man cleanse his way? By taking heed thereto according to Thy word.
>
> With my whole heart have I sought thee: O let me not wander from Thy commandments. Thy word have I hid in mine heart, that I might not sin against Thee.
>
> Psalm 119:9-11 (KJV)

NOTES

1. Jeane Westin, *The Coming Parent Revolution* (Chicago: Rand McNally & Co., 1981) (a summary of material in Chapter 14, entitled "The 'Wrongs' About Children's Sexual Rights.")
2. Marlee and Benny Alex, *You and Me and Our New Little Baby* (Grand Rapids: Zondervan Publishing House, 1982).
3. Maxine Hancock, *Confident Creative Children* (Chappaqua, New York: Christian Herald Books, 1981).
4. E. Margaret Clarkson, *Susie's Babies* (Grand Rapids: Wm. B. Eerdmans, 1960).
5. Marguerite Kurth Frey, *I Wonder, I Wonder* (St. Louis: Concordia Publishing House, 1967).
6. Grace Ketterman, M.D., *How to Teach Your Child About Sex* (Old Tappan, New Jersey: Fleming H. Revell Co., 1982).

8

Dating: A Spiritual Challenge

*With persuasive words she led him astray;
she seduced him with her smooth talk.*

Proverbs 7:21

If you thought it was tough to be a teenager in your own day, you should try walking in your teenager's shoes today! Adolescents are caught between the conservatism of their parents (and grandparents) and the philosophy of the sexual revolution that hits them from every direction.

Regardless where they go or what they do, they are bombarded with an overload of sexual information (really misinformation). If it's not in the magazines and newspapers, it's on television and in the movies. A ride down the street and you are accosted by seductive advertisements. Turn on the radio and the songs blare out their suggestive messages. Walk through a shopping mall and look at the titles of the best-selling books with their risque' jackets—you just can't get away from it.

Nothing is left to the imagination. One college student declared, "It can all be summed up in one word—liberation. We are supposed to be free from sexual hang-ups." The name of the dating game is self-fulfillment and gratification for those who are lured into and get caught in the sex trap.

When Should My Teenager Be Allowed to Date?

Parents want to know where they should go from here. "When should my teenager be allowed to date?" they ask wherever I go. It's a serious question when adolescents look years beyond their actual age and are exposed to so much more than you as parents were ever exposed to.

First of all, there are different kinds of dates. There are double dates, single dates, formal dates, and going-steady dates. Most of these are self-explanatory except perhaps formal dates. I describe this kind of dating as keeping later hours, which should generally be reserved for the more mature young man and woman. We aren't concerned with this kind of dating in this book, since we are dealing with adolescents.

Each of these kinds of dating implies different ages. Not everyone will be happy with my dating philosophy, but it's based on my own personal experience in counseling and working with families.

Double dates should be started in the tenth grade. I don't think young people are emotionally capable of handling dating before that. There's too much pressure in struggling with and adjusting to body changes. A date could be devastating and make things very difficult for them later on. Now I want to qualify this—I'm not so dumb as to think they're never going to go out together before the tenth grade. As one mother said, "My kids were always involved in a lot of coed-type things—youth meetings at church, camps, retreats—so they had lots of fun times with members of the opposite sex." That's generally the way it is, and this is good. But it's no fun to just hold hands at 16 if you've been "dating" the same girl since you were 13 or 14. Do you see what I mean? "Holding hands isn't fun anymore," I've had 16-year-olds tell me. The earlier they are allowed to date, the more temptation and pressures they face. I believe that parents can help protect their kids from this. They don't need any more temptation and pressure; they are already exposed to it from media blasts and all kinds of sources every day.

When your teenager reaches tenth grade or age 16, I believe this is an appropriate time to allow double dating. Each dating level should be a maturing passage. With more freedom comes more responsibility. The more freedom you give your teenager, the more responsibility you must lay on him. Another parent stated that she believed you had to respect the uniqueness of each child. Some kids are more mature than others and can handle responsibility. Some 16-year-olds can't handle it—they are irresponsible.

I'm also a firm believer in strict curfews. Depending on the maturity level of your teenager, single dating follows quite closely on the heels of some double dating. But no teenager is ready for dating until he understands what dating is all about, what proper behavior is, and the true meaning of life.

What Is Dating?

Dating is that time in life when young men and women 1) learn how to get to know persons of the opposite sex and 2) get to know one certain person of the opposite sex in a special way that prepares for engagement and marriage.[1]

I believe that dating should be fun. Initially when a fellow and a girl start dating there will be some tension, and that is to be expected; but dating gives teenagers opportunities to enjoy sports and activities together in a climate to know each other, to discover each other's tastes and previous life experiences. So in answer to the question, "What is dating?" I would have to say it is basically a special kind of socializing. "As we mature, our skills in interpersonal relationships, conversation, and understanding need to grow up with us. Dating is a terrific way to learn more about yourself, to become skilled at sensing the needs and feelings of another person, and to learn how to turn that insight into responsive action. Good dating prepares you for a happy, growing, and lasting marriage. Poor dating habits breed the fragile and short-lived marriages with which we're all too familiar."[2]

Josh McDowell and Paul Lewis in their important book, *Givers, Takers and Other Kinds of Lovers,* speak of the second key purpose of dating as being mate selection. Obviously, somewhere down the line (hopefully a long way down the line for teenagers), one of the persons dated will become the person he or she marries. Boy meets girl, girl meets boy, boy and girl date casually, boy and girl's relationship progresses to a beautiful, loving friendship, and on to steady dating, engagement, and marriage. That's a natural, healthy progression. But it doesn't always work that way. When insufficient time is invested in the relationship, and when the two people become involved in heavy petting and succumb to the sexual temptations, skipping over the cultivation of friendship and taking the time to really get to know the other person, the relationship will suffer. There's just no getting around it—nothing short-circuits a relationship and interpersonal communication like sexual exploitation, conquest, and a focus solely on the physical.

Parents can play an all-important role in helping their adolescent understand what dating is all about and can prepare him for this time of their life. This is where so many parents fall down in their training of the children whom God has entrusted to them. If only parents would come to grips with the necessity of helping their children and not back off through embarrassment or just plain indifference and neglect, assuming that their child understands. The two books from which I have quoted should be required reading for every parent. James Robison in *The Right Mate* emphasizes that the greatest mistake moms and dads make is to let their daughters and sons more or less drift into dating. I couldn't agree with him more. Why do we have this long, sad trail of broken homes across our nation, with confused, hurting children strewn along the way like so many discarded soft drink cans along highways? It comes partly from a careless attitude toward dating that has been perpetuated from one generation to another. Robison stresses that poor preparation for dating can lead to a lifetime of unfulfilled expectations, unhappiness, and misery. "For dating to be a wholesome, beneficial experience, a boy or girl must enter into it well fortified with certain basic truths and wide-awake to the danger of disregarding them."

Robison shows that one of the most important truths that young people must understand before dating is that a true concept of life is essential to a wholesome dating experience. Look at 1 John 1:3. The emphasis is on "fellowship with the Father and with his Son, Jesus Christ."

There is a very plain warning in 2 Corinthians 6:14,15 which says that we are not to be yoked together with unbelievers. "For what do righteousness and wickedness have in common? Or what fellowship can light have with darkness? What harmony is there between Christ and Belial? What does a believer have in common with an unbeliever?"

Fellowship with the Father is disrupted in our children when we allow them to become involved in a relationship with an unbeliever. Nothing could be more clear. And this *must* be made plain to teenagers *before* they begin dating. This is not to say that they ignore kids who are not Christians—the emphasis must always be on maintaining a good witness; we can't live in isolation. Friendship, yes, but not dating.

I get letters from kids all across the country where I've spoken in school assemblies. A lot of those letters concern this very thing. Here's a typical letter:

> Dear Rich,
>
> I'm 15 years old and there's a really neat guy at school who's a senior. Everybody likes him. He's also a great athlete. The problem is that he's not a Christian and he keeps asking me out. I'm a Christian and my parents are very much against me going out with him. I really want to go out with him, Rich, so that I can try to lead him to the Lord! Honest! Even my youth director at church doesn't take me seriously. What can I do?
>
> Signed, C.C.

In my reply I pointed her to a specific Old Testament command in which Moses told the people there was to be no intermarrying with those from other nations who did not know and serve God. Then there is the above-mentioned reference (2 Corinthians 6:14,15), which reinforces that command from the New Testament perspective. First Corinthians 7, speaking of a believer married to an unbeliever, states that she (or he) cannot leave the other when there are problems (*and there will be problems*). Remember, one of the two purposes of dating is to enable young men and women to meet and become friends with members of the opposite sex, and eventually this does lead to marriage.

I've had kids argue (and I know they do this with their parents) and say, "Look, I'm not planning to marry the guy—I just want to date him." Famous last words! Ask the woman who is married to an unbeliever; have her describe for you the agonies she has endured, the bitter pain, the disappointment, unfaithfulness, drinking, and involvement in a lifestyle that is entirely out of step with this girl's upbringing and Christian beliefs. And oh, the wasted years!

In responding to this girl, I showed her that we know God commands us to be faithful in witnessing to the lost (Mark 16:15), but God *never* contradicts Himself. If it was okay for a believer to date a nonbeliever just to have an opportunity to lead him to the Lord, would

God have said in His Word to us that we shouldn't be unequally yoked with unbelievers? No, of course not. We are to share our faith, but not in a dating situation, where we run the risk of becoming emotionally entangled in a romantic relationship.

I wrote to her:

> Going out on a date with an unsaved person would give him the wrong impressions and would put you in an awkward and vulnerable position. Remember, Jesus has your best interests in mind and He has your "perfect person" already selected. Don't blow His beautiful plan for your life by messing around with feelings that aren't aimed at doing His will. Be patient...remember, you are loved!

Another girl wrote a distressing letter in which she bared her heart:

Dear Rich:

> There is this guy at school that keeps bugging me. To be honest with you I used to date him. The problem is he is not a Christian. That's why I quit dating him in the first place. I'm really a very shy person and to have to keep saying "No" to this person is very difficult for me emotionally. I hope you don't mind me writing this letter, but I had to ask another Christian about this problem.

> Signed, G.O.

First of all, I'm going to make an observation. This girl should have been able to turn to her Christian parents for counsel. I don't know why they weren't available to her, but let's suppose it was a normal family situation—a Christian mom and dad. I want to tell you that there are an awful lot of kids out there being raised in homes like that; these kids don't feel they can turn to their parents. Parents, what's the matter with you? Why aren't *you* helping your kids through these dilemmas? I'm not trying to put a guilt trip on you, but I am trying to shock you enough to wake you up to the facts of life. In coming years you will wring your hands, cry your eyes out, spend a small fortune, and go through untold miseries when your sons and daughters have made poor choices in marriage. But you had it within your power to direct your teenagers' thinking so they wouldn't get into such a situation and foul up God's plan for their lives.

I wrote a letter commending this girl for having the good sense to break up the relationship. Then I pointed out the previously mentioned Scriptures to her, and shared with her that God is opposed to a believer dating or marrying a nonbeliever, and that when I was a staff pastor our church had a policy that we would only marry two Christians or two non-Christians, but never a Christian to a non-Christian.

Then I suggested that she sit down with the young man and explain her convictions. Here's what I said:

> Let him know that you answer to God for your relationships here on earth. If that doesn't sober him up, go to your principal and ask his assistance. I know this sounds harsh, but you are precious in God's sight and He wants to protect you. So you must care enough about yourself to protect yourself as well. Your actions toward this guy may help to increase the conviction of sin that he probably already feels from God.
>
> The second thing I want to talk to you about is your shyness. Did you know that shyness is really a form of pride? Being shy is really the result of not wanting anyone to reject you. Most shy people feel like if they don't open up, no one will ever have a reason to put them down. In other words, their pride won't allow them to be real. God made you, and like the great lady gospel singer once said, "God don't make no junk." That's true—He doesn't. Philippians 1:6 tells us that God isn't finished with us yet. I challenge you to lay your pride down and thank God for having made you (and for having done such a good job).

For a maximum relationship, our children must be taught that there must be a mutual and intimate communion on the deepest spiritual level. This should be a priority goal in all their dating so that whether the friend they are dating becomes someone about whom they get more serious as the friendship progresses, or whether that person remains just a good friend, it will be a mutually rewarding relationship blessed by God.

Raise the Standards

Parents sometimes say to me, "What do you do when the fellow your daughter is dating is someone you don't like?" This is not a trivial question. I tell parents, "Raise the standard." I'm not telling them to become legalistic, but I'm talking about being consistent parents. Establish the standard *before* they start dating, and then stick by it. What will that standard include?

In addition to the two purposes already mentioned for dating, and an explanation of the true concept of life, and a recognition of the Scriptural mandate, help your child to see that by simply asking questions he can quickly determine whether he should date a particular person or not.

1. How does this person line up with Scripture? As parents you can say, "We are a Bible-believing family. We've researched the standards by which we are going to live as a family, and in this area of dating, we want you to understand what Scripture says. We're not judging, nor are we attacking your friend, but we want you to understand the importance of dating someone whose character measures up to the Word of God." Then go through the Bible together, finding those places which speak of the Christian graces that should exemplify our lives.

2. Is this person you want to date someone who gets along well with other people? Is he/she fun to be around in a group situation? Explain that there are three aspects of the human personality: the intellect, the emotions, and the will. Before dating someone, your teenager should be acquainted well enough with this individual so that he can pick up clues as to his/her personality. The boy should be the spiritual leader even in a dating relationship, and if the boy does not show such spiritual understanding and is not interested in spiritual growth (through Bible study, prayer, and living according to Spiritual principles), your daughter must be helped to recognize that she is not to take it upon herself to remold the boy's life. That must come from within. Too many people enter into a relationship with a member of the opposite sex

with the idea in mind that they will change that person. That's not our prerogative; only God can transform a life. This can only result in bitter, unhappy pairing.

As two personalities interface, there must be a mutuality of interests. Our teenagers can be helped to look beyond the externals (the handsomeness of the boy and his athletic prowess or the beauty of the girl and her physical endowments) to the facets of personality that make a person distinct: attitudes, values, goals, likes, dislikes, idiosyncrasies. Of course these qualities don't always surface until dating has been going on awhile, but there should be enough clues initially so that once out on a date the girl wouldn't be put on the spot by the fellow saying, "Oh, by the way, we're going to Joe's Bar and Grill for some food and beer, and there's this neat rock group...."

Dating should be a fun time of life, but even in our fun we can line up with Scripture and not step out of the will of God. A prevalent attitude among teenagers today is that dating is for "making out." Welcome to the Land of Score, as one writer puts it. "What else is there to do?" they smirk.

Parents must teach their teenagers that boys are turned on by sight and girls by touch. Girls should be taught to dress modestly and in good taste. This doesn't rule out being fashionable, but it does rule out see-through blouses and slits in the skirts that come up to the navel! Our sons can be properly instructed so that while they extend the courtesies every female likes so well, they don't put the girl into a situation that becomes too hot to handle. Children are taught not to play with fire; in a broader sense that extends over into adolescence and dating. Josh McDowell and Paul Lewis say, "To wander carelessly and mindlessly into the potent arena of sex—letting your glands be your guide—is dangerous. It's *dumb*. Ignorantly wading into the swamp is a great way to find yourself up to your neck in alligators."

So we are to teach our children to exercise discernment. Show your teenagers the book of Proverbs often; read it at your family devotions. They can't help but notice the emphasis on being wise and discerning. In this whole arena of sexual promiscuity and its dangers and subtle allurements, have them read Proverbs 7 from *The Living Bible* or one of the other modern translations. Nothing could be more plain than words like these: "Listen to me, young men, and not only listen but obey; don't let your desires get out of hand" (verses 24, 25a, TLB).

Dating should be a fun way of providing a "climate in which two people can become friends," as McDowell and Lewis state so well. That rules out sitting in parked cars, backseat making-out, and movies in darkened theaters. "A good dating activity is one which helps you see and savor new delights and the depth of each other's personalities." Focus on just having fun together; there are lots of dating options. (See McDowell's and Lewis's book for several pages of fun things to do.)

Before leaving this subject, let me emphasize again the dangers of physical intimacy in the adolescent's dating experiences. This is a strong urge in the developing teenager, and parents *must* approach it with candor. One mother whose daughter got involved with an unbeliever has stated that if she could only undo the years, she would take her beautiful daughter aside and say, "I love you too much not to be 100 percent open and honest with you, honey. I can't allow you to throw your life away in a relationship that I know will only hurt you in the end." Then she said she would explain what could happen just as a result of even a little intimacy involving touching. At risk of embarrassing herself and her daughter, she wouldn't omit anything. That's one mother's feelings. She said much more, but you mothers reading this get the idea. Fathers should be able to communicate these same ideas to their sons; and if you are a mother reading this who doesn't have the backup support of a husband, then take it upon yourself to level with that kid of yours.

One way to level with adolescents is to affirm them. "I know you are too intelligent to mess up your life by getting involved in a situation that could cause you lots of heartache."

Another way to affirm a teenager is to say, "I like your choice of friends. He/she is intelligent" (or whatever asset you choose to focus on).

Teenagers need to hear that they are loved and appreciated. "I'm really proud of you. Do you know how much your dad and I love you?" Such affirmations should work to bring out the best in your child. They *want* to live up to your expectations. Along this line, you may want to read Anne Ortlund's book *Children Are Wet Cement.*

The reason I've spent so much time on this subject is because of the letters I receive from teenagers and from the heartbreaking conversations I have with the parents of these kids in trouble or with adolescents who apparently aren't getting much direction from their parents. Here's one such letter.

Dear Rich:

I've just finished high school and my boyfriend is a sophomore in college. We've both been very active in the youth ministry of our church. Recently my boyfriend asked me to marry him and I said yes. We both know it's God's will. We've never gone "all the way" before, but certainly have moved beyond the "kissing stage." Rich, in your opinion, what would be wrong with two Christian young people, who are getting married anyway, going "all the way" before marriage?

Signed, F.F.

Here's my response:

Dear F.F.,

I will not fall into the trap of giving you my opinion, but I will tell you what the Bible says. Sexual intercourse before marriage is wrong and is called fornication. Read Genesis 39:9; Matthew 15:19; Colossians 3:5; 1 Corinthians 6:9; Galatians 5:19,21; Revelation 21:8.

I feel like you're asking another question as well. Maybe you're wanting to know just how far you can go short of intercourse before marriage. A good rule to follow is that those activities which have their natural end in intercourse (i.e., "heavy making-out" or "petting") should be out of the question. Paul said in Romans 14:13,21 that we should not do anything that would cause our brother or sister in the Lord to stumble. When in doubt about a certain activity, DON'T! Romans 14:23 says, "Everything that does not come from faith is sin." If you can't see in your mind's eye Jesus smiling on your physical relationship before marriage, then you can be sure the Holy Spirit is wanting you to hold back for the sake of your relationship with each other and the Lord.

I'm not saying that you're not going to relate to each other physically before marriage. I'm not dumb! But I do believe that when the Holy Spirit says to wait, it's always for something better. If you will remain pure and holy before God prior to marriage, your trust in each other's commitment will provide the sexual happiness in marriage that you're desiring. Being a young Christian bride-to-be, you probably already know that you are loved.

Then there was a letter from a college student that really tore my heart, and shows what can happen when fellows and girls overstep the bounds.

Dear Rich:

I'm a Christian female college student. This past year I met a tremendous Christian guy, I thought. After months of dating he asked me to marry him. I accepted with my parents' full approval. At the time he had not yet purchased the ring. My fiance, had to leave for several months to work in another state. He told me he loved me very much and that when he returned he would bring the ring. He also led me into sexual sin. I repented when he left. When he came home he told me the ring he had gotten in the other state was too small for me so he was going to take it back and exchange it. We sinned again before he went back. He's been gone for three weeks and last night he told me on the phone that he didn't think it was God's will that we get married, so now he's going to join the Marines.

Rich, I totally feel ripped off and hurt and used. I feel like my life is over and that God will never take me back after what I've done with this guy. Thanks for reading this and offering your advice.

Signed G.C.

My reply:

Dear G.C.:

You can't change the past! Sin carries its own consequences. You chose selfishly and you're having to bear the responsibility for your fornication. However, God forgives. Why don't you let Him forgive you (1 John 1:9)? Receive His forgiveness and get on with your life (John 10:10).

Also, you are an individual that God wants to use. Try not to let your whole purpose in life be to find a guy. When it's right, God will bring that person into your life. You won't have to *struggle* and *fret* and *worry* . It will be a perfectly natural thing and you will know it (read Genesis 24). I'm praying for you in this matter and remember, you're loved.

In summing this up, parents, be tough if you have to when helping your child to see that God is the One who has set the standard, and that we as His children (if we really claim to belong to Him) *will obey* that standard. Then our children won't get caught in the kind of situation which the girl who wrote that heartbreaking letter found herself in. If they *do* get caught, when they're backed by your prayers (which you can assure your teens they always have when they're dating) they can resist the temptation. We are never left powerless when we are relying on God to help us.

Get to Know Your Teenager's Dates

It's not fair for you as parents to make a judgment about your teenager's choice of dates if *you* haven't made some effort to get to know that fellow or girl. That's what your kids are going to say to you, and they are right. I know that's difficult, but I believe very strongly in controlled situations. We owe this to our adolescents. Encourage your son or daughter to invite his/her friends over to the house. I know some parents who put a pool in their backyard just so they could maintain control. "It was an expensive thing to do," the father said, and the mother chimed in, "But what a terrific investment!" Each then elaborated on that—they were investing in their children's relationships. The pool would help make it possible for the kids to spend time at home with their friends. *They* would be in control.

Our neighborhood was the controlled situation that my parents wanted it to be when I was growing up. Our yard was the play center. My father was a nut for a neat yard, but he gave it all up when I got to the age where he knew I needed control. We've had as many as fifteen guys out in that yard playing football with just about as many gals watching from the sidelines. I mean, it was controlled!

All the tents of the neighborhood were camped in our backyard. Some people go out and buy their family a boat and water skis. They are investing so they can control the situation. "Well," you protest, "I don't want to spend the money." Do you want to keep your eye on your kids? Maybe you can't afford to do some of these things, but make sure you know who your teenagers' friends are.

Invite them over to your house for dinner or for after-church fellowship. Ask your daughter (or son) to point out to you that special fellow (or gal) in whom she (he) is interested. Then make it a point to get to know him (her) while he (she) is at your home. Make certain that this person also learns something about your family and your daughter (or son). "Karen really loves the Lord. We are proud of her. We're sold out for the Lord." The idea is you want this young person to know that your family has a strong commitment to Biblical standards. This also works in another way: it puts the monkey on your child's back. If he doesn't live what you've told other people he's living, in his friends' sight he's going to look like a hypocrite.

I believe teenagers need some pressure like that. Too many parents are always trying to take the pressure off. That's a mistake. Don't kid yourself—these kids can handle pressure. You'd be surprised at how strong they are. Give them something to live up to. Set those standards high, and don't ever lower them.

NOTES

1. James Robison, *The Right Mate* (Wheaton: Tyndale House Publishers, 1979), p. 27.
2. Josh McDowell and Paul Lewis, *Givers, Takers and Other Kinds of Lovers* (Wheaton: Tyndale House Publishers, 1980), pp. 94-95.

9

When the Drug Problem Hits Home

He who scorns instruction will pay for it,
but he who respects a command is rewarded.
                                    Proverbs 13:13

One of the most crushingly sad things I encounter is parents whose kids are strung out on mind-altering drugs or on alcohol. The helplessness and the trauma that this inflicts upon parents is almost indescribable. If ever there was an influence that is antifamily, it has to be this drug epidemic in our nation. Sadly, there are many parents—including Christian parents—who refuse to admit that *their* kid could have *this* kind of problem. But I want to tell you the problem is here, it's real, and it's no respecter of persons (or Christian families). I have to tell parents, "Get your heads out of the sand, become informed, be aware of what the danger signals are, and then if you do have a son or daughter hooked on drugs, *immediately* take steps to do what *has* to be done."

How to Detect Drug Addiction

One high school teacher says, "I can always tell the kids who are on pot because they have such bad memories. They forget the beginning of a sentence before they finish it."[1] Parents, does that ring any bells with you?

I tell parents three signs to watch for in particular that *might* indicate their kids are using drugs. (Notice my emphasis on the word *might*. It doesn't necessarily mean they *are* on drugs, but if your son or daughter shows these symptoms, especially all of them, then you need to investigate without further delay.)*

Evasion of Responsibility

The drug user is a person who will evade responsibility. It's not that he doesn't want to work, but he seems to forget. He seems to be displaced. He easily forgets orders that were given. His work just never seems to get done.

In this area of evading responsibility, attendance at school may be a factor that is affected. Watch his school attendance. Call his counselor. Make it a point to find out if he's been skipping classes. If he isn't in class, let me tell you he isn't out studying behind the mulberry bush! School is the place where the connections are made to obtain drugs, especially for younger adolescents.

Another thing to watch for is disappearance—he will disappear at unusual times for unexplained lengths of time with strange explanations. A young druggy is very irresponsible and just disappears easily; he doesn't think about the family dinner hour. "Son, we've always eaten at 6:00 o'clock. Where have you been?" "Oh, I didn't know that," he'll respond as he comes dragging in at 8:00 o'clock expecting supper.

We had a young fellow living with us one time who had been struggling with drugs. We wanted to help him, so we took him under our wings. He would come straggling in at the weirdest hours and then offer flimsy excuses. Did he think I was born in a barn? But druggies will come up with some strange excuses and think nothing of it. If

* Narcotics Education, Inc., 6830 Laurel Street, NW, Washington, DC 20012, has a brochure entitled *The Parents' Guide to Drug Abuse*. This lists eight signs to look for: 1) a tendency to sit looking off into space; 2) laughing excessively at things that are funny only to him; 3) an appearance of intoxication with no odor of alcohol; 4) staying out later than usual and giving evasive answers when questioned; 5) avid reading about things connected with the drug culture; 6) loss of appetite, perhaps with a rapid loss of weight; 7) the reverse—an increase in appetite with wild forays on the cupboards and refrigerator. However, these may also be symptoms of other physical or emotional difficulties, so don't panic too soon. The Health Insurance Institute of New York offers one way to clarify the situation: 8) make a close inspection of the youngster's eyes. For example, one giveaway would be a fluctuation in the width of the pupils not accounted for by changes in light. You may want to write for this brochure.

they weren't under the influence of the drugs, they would be embarrassed to say such ridiculous things.

Physical Changes

Pot, which is the most-used drug in schools, will usually produce red eyes. That's an up-front, easily identifiable sign. Also, there will be an unusual smell—it's like they haven't put on any cologne or used deodorant for days because the smell of the weed gets in their clothes. It's a strange, foreign kind of smell. So check the smells in their bedroom. I know that sounds odd, but I know of no other way to put it to make it really plain. If they're burning candles a lot, they're probably trying to disguise the smell. (They've been told by their friends that the candle smell will dispel the pot smell.) They'll try to excuse themselves and throw you off guard with "Oh, I just like the smell of candles, Mom."

Along with physical changes comes moodiness. Pill-poppers and pot-smokers are subject to pronounced moodiness. If you find your teenager in a more moody frame of mind than usual—a detached sort of feeling when you try to relate to him—check it out. Don't just cast this aside as a temporary thing your kid is going through. Start being concerned about it.

One of the terms that young people use to describe what happens under the influence of drugs is "spaced out." You can detect it when they seem to have a distant, faraway look, with everything just wandering—their eyes, their thoughts—when you try to talk to them. It's as if they're in another world while you're trying to communicate with them. They're spaced out.

There will also be a lower energy level. Even the stimulants they take won't keep them from depression, because when they come down from the stimulants there's a heavier depression that sets in.

"Large amounts of marijuana," says Dr. Sidney Cohen, former head of the National Institute on Drug Abuse, "have a depressant effect upon the central nervous system...[and] produce a decreased desire to work, poor performance and a blunted emotional response."

One of the tragedies about drug use relates to the long-term effects. One physician specializing in adolescent care, Dr. Walter X. Lehmann, contends that some of these young people never make it all the way back, even if they quit smoking marijuana. "I know a lot of young people," he says, "who have broken the pot habit and seem to be doing well, but who are not likely to realize the rich potential that once was theirs."[2]

What a waste of human potential! And to think that this is what some people want to legalize in this country and to accept as a "rite of passage—just experimental high jinks."

Let me explain to you the term "wasted." When a person is using marijuana, its major active ingredient is delta-9-tetrahydrocannabinol (THC), which doesn't dissipate with the marijuana's sweet-smelling smoke. It stays in the person's body, burrowing into brain and body tissues, where it accumulates. So if this kid is putting 5, 10, 15, 20, or more joints into his body in one week, he's never able to eliminate the residue from his system. It's always lingering. It's always pulling at his energy level. As much as he wants to get himself together, he just can't. There's just this lowered energy level. He kind of droops his way through life.

Don't ever let anyone tell you that marijuana is just an exotic herb. My research tells me that it contains 419 chemicals, 61 of them found in no other plant! Who knows what risks these kids are subjecting their bodies to for years to come, and what effect this may have on the children they have! The National Institute on Drug Abuse and ongoing studies by the Department of Health and Human Services show that heavy pot use can alter chromosomes and produce lower sperm counts. (I'll have more to say on marijuana since it is the one drug that the drug culture glorifies the most.)

Rebellion

In drug use there's a general coldness in your relationship that develops—a hardness, an alienation. It's as if your words hit them in the face and bounce off. It's as if your kids are a wall or a rock. It's an icy indifference that you can't cut through. That warmth you once received from them is gone. "Hi, Dad! Hi, Mom!" That spontaneity of delight in seeing you is missing.

They become liars. A druggie is a liar. He can look you in the face and lie without blinking an eye. Your sweet little child who wouldn't hurt a flea will turn out lying like the devil. You wince. Yes, I know that it hurts to read this. Parents, I'm deadly serious about this. They become profuse liars. They have to lie—there's no way they can be truthful and keep this thing covered up. Their whole lifestyle becomes altered. But parents want to believe their kids and end up believing their lies and the cover-up to which they resort. "Oh, Mom, you know I'd never use drugs."

Mom says, "But what about those pills I found in your pocket?"

"Mom, those were Cindy's. She was having cramps and didn't have a pocket on her so she asked me to keep them in case she needed them between classes." And Mom ends up believing her innocent-looking daughter.

We want to trust our kids. We know it's important to them to believe that we have confidence in them. We've also been hooked into this "Kids have rights too" philosophy, and we don't want to be labeled as being snoopy parents. But what about parents' rights? Jeane Westin (*The Coming Parent Revolution*), in her interviews with parents, asked: If you thought your child had drugs or alcohol in his or her room, would you think you had the right to search it? Sixty-two percent said yes and 38 percent no, but many of the "yes" parents weren't happy at the thought. A Mississippi mother of three explained: "Once I thought I couldn't—the sacredness of privacy and trust and all that— but after searching my daughter's room, I feel no guilt about it. She wasn't being honest with me and was endangering her health."[3]

Other parents agreed, confident in their right to protect their children. Mrs. Westin makes an interesting point: "A funny thing about the right to privacy—children often confuse it with a right to be secret, to hide things they think parents aren't supposed to know about. It's perfectly natural to want privacy, but when drugs or alcohol are involved in adolescent secretiveness, it is all too often accompanied by withdrawal from the family. A parent runs the risk of losing a withdrawn child." She quotes actress and comedienne Carol Burnett, whose teenage daughter, Carrie, became involved in drugs, and who said, "I was a snoop, and I am very glad I was. You *have* to know what you're dealing with. You always read, 'No, let your kids have their privacy.' Well, I say, *snoop!*"[4]

Parents whose kids are on drugs have learned the hard way that discipline doesn't seem to affect them in the least. They've tried withholding privileges, detaining them—some have even tried the seat of the hand to the bottom of the anatomy (even on their teens)—but nothing works. The kid walks out on a session with his parents—just boldly gets up and takes off. Parents are left shouting, "Wait a minute! I'm in charge here!" Oh, really? Rebellion becomes more noticeable with an I-don't-give-a-hoot attitude on the part of the kid. The kid knows he's got his parents in a bind—he knows they don't want to kick him out, because that sure won't solve the problem, so he thinks he has them over a barrel. What's a parent supposed to do? That brings us to the next decisive issue in this whole area of coping with the drug problem when it hits home.

How to Respond to Your Child Using Drugs

Increasingly, across the country, parents are being galvanized into action by the drug explosion that is affecting younger and younger children yearly, and turning some of them into "vegetables," according to drug counselors and those in the know.

Some of these kids are first discovered using drugs when their parents suspected they were being ripped off by children needing money, and the kids would come up with some way-out reasons for requiring extra cash. Be sure you know where the money you give your kids is going. That's not too much to expect—you have a right to know. After all, who's putting in the long hours to earn the bucks? And don't forget that drug users become expert liars. I don't want to turn you into a Sherlock Holmes-type investigative parent, but it's better to be labeled a penny pincher or whatever your child chooses to call you than to discover too late that you were financing their destructive habit.

One group of Atlanta parents who decided to band together and to use their combined parental muscle to monitor their kids were called by their children "The Anti-drug Nosey Parents Association." So be it—they dared to be authoritative, take-charge-type parents, and dared to take action.

Here's what I tell parents must be done.

1. *Don't ignore drug use ever again. Believe that the problem exists. Get smart.*

Some parents are just totally dumb. Ignorant. Some of them are willfully so. They are the heads-stuck-in-the-sand-type I referred to earlier. *Their* kid just wouldn't do such a thing! Some of these parents act like this drug epidemic is happening in Missouri, or California, or wherever—but certainly not in *their* state and town. Others are ignorant of the facts simply because they are uninformed. They may not be reading current magazine or newspaper articles dealing with the problem; they may be ignoring the latest news reports. For one reason or another the seriousness of the drug problem has escaped their attention. But I want to tell you, friends, it's happening, and it's happening here—wherever you are reading this right now. It's happening!

Associated Press released a news item stating that there are at least 310,000 heroin addicts in 16 major U.S. cities and only about 25 percent of them are receiving treatment (*Fort Worth Star Telegram*, June 11, 1982). Congressional officials are predicting a crime wave the magnitude of which we have never experienced before in this country as a result of alcohol and drug abuse nationwide. Of course, addicted people need money to support their habits; many of them are so addicted that they are unable to hold down jobs. So what do they do? They resort to theft and crime.

I read about two young people in the same household in Cleveland, Ohio, who paid a friend 60 dollars to kill their father. The boy came over with a .38 caliber pistol and blew his friends' father's brains out. The 17-year-old brother and 14-year-old sister took off with their friend who did the shooting. But they didn't take off without first taking their father's wallet—he had just been paid and they knew it. They went on a two-week spending spree, not even feeling guilty, before the police caught up with them. Why did they have their father killed? Because they wanted to smoke pot and he disapproved. One figure says that 33 percent of young people ages 12 to 17 are hooked on pot in this country. Sixty-three percent of America's 18-to-25 age group use pot. And 20 percent of those over 25 use marijuana.

The previously mentioned survey of 16 major cities included Baltimore, Boston, Buffalo, New York, Chicago, Cleveland, Detroit, Jersey

City, Kansas City, Los Angeles, Minneapolis, Philadelphia, Providence (Rhode Island), San Antonio, San Francisco, and Washington. But the figures are at best only estimates since drug use is illegal and many addicts are undetected. This same report said that the greatest unmet need in detection and treatment is among adolescent alcohol and drug abusers. So parents, don't sit there and think it can't happen to your child. Don't ignore drug use. Believe that the problem exists and that it could affect your child. Get smart.

2. *Learn all you can about the nature of drugs.*

Read. Become informed. Attend lectures and films offered by your community, church, or school. Go to your local library. Check out books on drug abuse. Know the signs. Memorize them. Sit down with your family and teach them about the dangers of drugs—even your children in elementary school need to know this. Maybe I should say *especially* your younger children. I've read and heard about children as young as seven and eight being hooked on drugs.

The Atlanta parents previously mentioned had been advised by experts that there wasn't much they could do but wait it out. They had learned that their sixth- and seventh-grade children were casually smoking pot and viewing it as "no big deal." But these are the actions they took.

a. They contacted the parents of all their children's friends and told them that parents were forming a group to find out if there was a drug problem.

b. They met to pool their information. They aired suspicions, rumors, gossip, and guesses, as well as known facts. They even determined to find out which friends of each other's children were involved as users and suppliers and confronted *their* parents.

c. They educated themselves on the effects of drugs and on the local drug scene. They involved the help of local family service and drug counseling agencies. Sometimes you may find that the professionals are uninterested or passive, and if that's the case, be prepared to do your own education research.

d. They committed themselves to teaching drug and alcohol facts at home.

e. They took a firm stand, clearly opposing any drug use by their children.

f. They evolved a common code of basic behavior for drugs, dating, curfews, and chaperoning. Then they presented a unified parental front. (I think this is very significant and will go a long way to diffuse the drug problem in a local community—*a unified parental front.*)

g. They kept a parent-communication network open. (This is closely aligned to the above, but I believe it should be emphasized as an all-important step for concerned parents to take.)

These parents were very wise; they recognized that their kids would fight to maintain their circle of friends and that they would be sullen, defiant, and deceptive. What the Atlanta parents emphasized was that parents have to hang in there together so that the kids recognize their seriousness.

h. They worked hard at developing fun and constructive alternatives to drug use in the community. (This, too, I believe to be vital. It's one thing to say a kid can't do something and/or participate with friends in an activity, but good psychology has always dictated that if you take something away, you need to replace it with something better.)[5]

This is, in effect, parents banding together to counter youth peer pressure. This is very effective.

3. *Don't overreact, but set standards.*

Maybe you haven't had verbal precedents before in your family. Well, don't walk around saying "If only...." Get busy and set standards and precedents *now*. Hand-wringing and weeping profusely isn't going to change the situation. Sure, you'll do that too, but *now* is the time for take-charge parenting. But I must caution you about overreacting. Keep control—of yourself and them and the difficult circumstances.

Remember too that this is going to take time. Your kid didn't get hooked on drugs overnight. I must caution you about overreacting by exploding. Exploding isn't going to be any better than the emotional reaction of hand-wringing and weeping. The situation isn't going to change overnight.

Get your own act together as parents. Get smart. Learn what you can as fast as you can, and then decide on your approach. One thing you may elect to do as soon as possible is to get counseling. Is your pastor or youth pastor qualified to help in this area? If not, find out who in your community is. Search out that help. And don't be so full of pride that you can't admit that you and your kid need help.

Do what the Atlanta parents did—join or start a parent-action group to help fight drug abuse in your schools and in your community. Dr. Harold Voth, senior psychiatrist at the Menninger Foundation, insists that "Someone who cares must intervene totally, consistently, and with unrelenting perseverance. Efforts short of all-out efforts generally fail."

Now those are strong words. And if your child is *really hooked* on drugs, Dr. Voth believes the child must be removed from his culture for a minimum of three months. I've read and seen interviews on TV where the parents did this very thing. It was hard. It was really difficult to take their kid out of school, to admit publicly in this way that the child had this monstrous problem, but they've done it and the kid has been helped. It takes a lot of parental love and sacrifice. But this is real love.

There is a difference between psychological and physical dependence on drugs. Both require strong spiritual support. But let's say your child is just getting involved in drugs and you've made the discovery. You set the standards by putting the fear of God in their hearts, and I'm 100 percent in favor of this. It's Biblical. What more can I say? Do we want to save our children from the pit of hell or don't we care?

4. *Instruct them in what the Bible says.*

Some of your children are heavily into drugs. My heart aches with you. You've told me, "Rich, we've been struggling with this for a long time. They are chronic dope users. We don't know what to do. We think we've helped them for a time, only to discover that they've slipped back into it. We don't know what to do."

Regardless of where you are with your children on the scale—just into drugs, heavy on drugs, or worried that they may succumb to peer pressure and get involved—you must let your child know, "I'm really serious about this. Drug usage is wrong. It's going to rip you off. And because I love you so much, and because I care more than I can possibly tell you, I am going to become involved on a greater scale than just with our family's concern. I'm going to make a stink about it and everyone is going to know that your mother and father are *advocates against drugs*." That's a beginning approach.

This may shock your child, but he needs to be shocked. No one likes to be embarrassed, but once the child realizes that you mean business and that your involvement in the community is for real, he may step back and do some serious thinking.

But you must move beyond that. Has your child heard you pray about his situation? If you have to get up at 6:00 in the morning to agonize about your son or daughter to get your point across, then do it. Don't do it for show and to impress your child, but do it because you mean business with God. I mean PRAY audibly—let your petitions be known to your heavenly Father. You have not because you ask not. "Oh God, help Tom with his drug problem." Bring God into this agony. "Father, my daughter has a drug problem. Oh God, help my precious child."

This is a spiritual problem, my friend, and you need all the resources of heaven working on your behalf. But in the process, don't cut your child off. Give that precious child your full emotional support—love, acceptance, forgiveness. Keep those lines of communication open.

J.C. Ryle, the great Bible expositor, in speaking of prayer uses the illustration of the needle-grinders of Sheffield, who sometimes wore magnetic mouthpieces at their work to catch all the fine dust that flew around them, to prevent it from entering their lungs. Prayer is the mouthpiece you must wear continually, or else you will never work uninjured by the unhealthy atmosphere of this world. *You must pray. And you must let your child know that you love him, accept him, and forgive him unconditionally.*

Then you must instruct him in what the Bible says about drugs. And it does have something to say. When speaking of drugs, the Bible uses the terms "sorcery" and "enchantments." "Sorcery" comes from the Greek word *pharmakia,* a drug. It's the word from which we get our word "pharmacy," which of course means the art or profession of preparing and dispensing drugs and medicine. Ancient witches used drugs in their practice of sorcery and witchcraft. In Scripture, drugs are related to witchcraft. God is against it! Here are a few Scriptures that our young people need to know about.

Deuteronomy 18:9-13	Here anyone who engages in sorcery, witchcraft, or casting spells is called detestable in the sight of the Lord, and these are labeled ''detestable practices.''
2 Kings 17:7-23	Speaks of the people of Israel being exiled because of sinful practices (including sorcery).
Jeremiah 27:9	Warns against sorcery.
Isaiah 47:9	Speaks of the disaster that comes upon those who trust in sorceries, potent spells, and wickedness.
Acts 8:9-24	Tells of Simon the sorcerer who was ''captive to sin.'' When he ran into the power of God, Simon recognized that his sorcery couldn't hold a candle to the power that the apostle Peter had, which came from God.
Acts 13:6-12	Speaks of a sorcerer running into the power of God.
Revelation 21:8	Those who practice magic arts and who turn aside from following God are headed for hell.

When I speak to young people I unhesitatingly tell them they can't smoke dope and serve Jesus. I get letters like this:

Dear Rich:

I smoke pot and still believe that I am going to heaven. I read my Bible and pray. I always smoke pot in a private place and never with other people. Lately I've had strange feelings about this, like maybe it's wrong. Now I'm really mixed up; I thought maybe you knew something about this problem.

Signed, S.I.

In my speaking and in my letter replies I tell the kids that God is against sensual drug usage. When witches used drugs on their patients it was to create a "high," and then the person would have unusual faith in the witch. Strange healings were sometimes performed through the patient's unusual faith in the Devil. But it began with the drug-induced high. (Then I give them the above Scriptures.)

I also give them some facts about marijuana and other drugs, including alcohol. (Those facts are readily available to anyone who wants to take the time to learn them. I have already given some facts in this chapter.) I tell them, among other things, that cannabis is the botanical name for the hemp plant, the source of marijuana. The drug comes as a resinous wax, and when crudely separated it is called "hashish." This resin was and still is used as a pesticide. It drives insects and bugs crazy. Oddly enough, it's doing the same thing to humans. (I also speak to them of THC, previously explained in this chapter.) Doctors have discovered that repeated use of marijuana will affect your brain functions and will damage your liver, respiratory system, endocrine system, and other body cells. Read 1 Corinthians 6:19,20.

Why is God against smoking pot or any other kind of drug usage for sensual reasons? Here's the answer: drugs remove a person's mind from reality, with a loss of control. When a person gives himself over to a drug "high," the Devil will in turn fill the person's head with his garbage without the person even knowing it.

The guilt that this young person wrote about was not just because he had broken God's law, but also because the Devil had been dumping his filth into his head while he was "high." I remind young people that God is so against this kind of sin that he says in Revelation 21:8 that drug dealers, users, and abusers will be sent to hell.

Parents, I believe when the drug problem hits home, you've got to get brutally honest with your kids. Put some holy fear into them. Remember, you are saving them from the very pit of hell. I believe it. I preach it. You'd better do it too.

Before leaving this subject, I want to emphasize to you the necessity for you to teach your children thoroughly, to instruct them according to the Word of God in these things, and then to be a good listener to what they are saying back to you. Listen also to what they are listening to on the radio and on TV. Who are their heroes? What are their heroes and heroines singing and saying to them? The songs they are hearing are pushing the goodness of drugs.

Say to your child, "You know that song that talks about how good it feels to get high on drugs; I was listening to that today. Honey, do you listen to that often? How does that song strike you?" Don't immediately outright condemn the song; give your child a chance to respond. I guarantee that it will freak your child out if they hear you showing *that* kind of interest in him.

Then give him the facts. You've become an informed parent. You're smart now. You're not overreacting, but you're instructing your child in the truth. Maybe he's never honestly been confronted with the truth in this way. Who better to give it to him than you, the parent in charge? Show him the futility and danger of succumbing to peer pressure, and then level with him with the open Word of God in your hands. "Son, we are a Christian family. Here's what God says.... Son, we love you too much to allow you to wreck your life this way. Jeremiah 33:3 says, 'Call to me and I will answer you.' This is what we need to do together. James 4:7,8 says, 'Submit yourselves, then, to God. Resist the devil, and he will flee from you. Come near to God and He will come near to you.' "

Parents, let me encourage you. Turn this drug problem over to the Lord. It's not your problem alone. Parents all over America are in this thing with you. But remember, your child is God's child. God loves this child more than you do. God's grace is sufficient for you in this hour of your great need. Draw upon His grace, and in so doing your child will see a parent with a new and beautiful attitude and with a strength that he can fall back on.

NOTES

1. Westin, *The Coming Parent Revolution,* p. 236.
2. Ibid.
3. Ibid., p. 244.
4. Ibid., pp. 244-45.
5. Ibid., pp. 240-41.

10

What Do I Do When I've Lost My Authority?

*He who brings trouble on his family will inherit
only the wind.*

                              Proverbs 11:29

"Don't panic!" Have you heard those words before? Have you said
them to yourself in the dark of night when your pillow is wet with
tears? Have you been hanging on for dear life but feel that you're about
to lose your grip? Some of you reading this bought the book just for
this chapter. In thumbing through you came across the title. You know
it was meant just for you. You know you've lost your authority. You
suspect you may have lost your much-loved son or daughter for good.
Your heart is breaking. You wonder if there are any more tears to be
shed.

Regardless of where I go, I encounter parents like you. Their children
have thrown all the rules out the window; they feel they've lost their
chances with a son or daughter forever. They know they've blown
it for good. "It's over," they tell me as they dab at their eyes with
a soggy Kleenex. I'm writing this to tell you it's never over. It's never
too late. As long as there's life, there's hope.

There are several reasons why relationships with our adolescents
suffer. Sometimes it's big things like getting involved with the wrong
crowd, getting started on drugs and drinking, or a too-heavy and
premature relationship with a member of the opposite sex. At other
times it's a form of mild rebellion against parental authority and what
the kids claim are too many restrictions. These differences can vary
in severity. Most of the time it results in the child turning his back
on his parents and on God. This also means a turning away from the
church and its spiritual leaders. Concerned parents are keenly disap-

pointed and deeply concerned. Many fear it's too late to do anything, but over and over I hear, "Do you have any suggestions as to what we can do?"

Retrace Your Steps

At this stage it does little good to try to assess blame, so I'm not going to lay a guilt trip on you. Nevertheless, if parents are to be helped in coping with this problem, and if their children's lives are to be salvaged, then first of all they must stop pitchforking the blame off onto the school, the child's peers, the church, the society, or even the Devil. Even if the parents have been diligent in the training and instruction of their children, to refuse to acknowledge their part in this problem and to do a little self-examination is to compound the problem. This may be a painfully honest thing to do, but it is essential.

I tell parents they need to retrace their steps. Go back in your mind to when you believe the relationship with your teenager began to erode. How did it begin? What precipitated the differences? Who was involved? What was said? Take a pad and pencil and write these things down if it will help. Fathers and mothers need to sit down together and think this through. If you honestly can't pinpoint it, then you need to ask your teenager if he can remember what it was that contributed to making the relationship suffer. Other family members may need to be included in this discussion. But it's important to try hard to get at the root cause.

Along this line, you as parents may need to ask yourself questions like these: Were we too authoritarian? Were we too indulgent? Were we overprotective? Have we given enough time to our troubled teenager? Have we failed to meet needs that were less obvious than providing clothing, food, and material needs? You may need to bare your hearts and say to your teenager, "How have we failed you? What have we done to cause this alienation?" Or you may need to say, "We've been too indulgent; we haven't followed through on responsibilities that we've given you. We've hindered rather than helped you. Now we've got to lay some new rails and we're all going to have to work together to keep on the track."

Forgive As He Forgives

I can remember an occasion when I made a bad mistake in my young life due to some information my father gave me that was incorrect. When I realized that he was in error, I couldn't wait to get home and rip him to shreds. I was going to really lay it on him. This was one time when I had it over him. I was going to be able to show him he wasn't always right. I was actually happy about it all. When I arrived home, I burst into the house and said, "Man, Dad, you sure gave me some wrong information—" but before I could go any further my dad said, "Hey, I'm really sorry. I realized after you left that I didn't have the right information. Can you forgive me?"

Talk about the wind going out of my sails! I had all these guns ready to fire at him with heavy artillery when he says, "I'm sorry...forgive me." Now the monkey was on my back. There wasn't going to be any war.

"Well, ur...uh...okay. Just don't do it again...." I learned an important lesson right then and there. There's nothing quite like saying "I'm sorry" to diffuse someone's anger or bad feelings. My dad stood tall in my eyes as a result of that experience. We're seldom so big in the eyes of our children as when we admit our fallibility.

Parents whose teenagers are alienated from them may need to ask forgiveness for some problem that's of long duration. It shouldn't have gone unresolved this long, but you may not even have been aware of it. That's why it's important to retrace your steps.

Forgive as He forgives. Since God in Christ has forgiven us so much, how can we possibly withhold forgiveness from those who have offended us in whatever way! In a previous chapter I mentioned the importance of holy living. The reference is to be found in Hebrews 12:14,15: "Make every effort to live in peace with all men and to be holy; without holiness no one will see the Lord. See to it that no one misses the grace of God and that no bitter root grows up to cause trouble and defile many." Withholding forgiveness results in bitterness taking root. This is very important for adolescents to learn. As long as they fail to learn the beautiful Christian grace of forgiving, they risk alienation and becoming bitter and cynical.

As parents we also need to forgive ourselves for real or imagined failure in our relations with our children. When you have a less-than-ideal relationship with your adolescent, the first thing to do is to reach out to him, to retrace your steps, to admit you may have goofed, to be willing to forgive and to accept someone else's plea for forgiveness, and to forgive yourself.

A word of caution is in order. Dr. Bruce Narramore warns about seeking to solve problems with our teenagers only out of underlying guilt feelings. We must have more than our own feelings in mind, since an adolescent can spot phoniness. Our concern must not be just to relieve our own anxiety, but the greater welfare of our child.

There is another important principle that both parents and their children must come to grips with, and it relates to forgetful forgiveness. Proverbs 17:9 tells us that love forgets mistakes. Our example is our heavenly Father. David, who committed a grievous sin with another man's wife, knew what it was to experience this kind of forgiveness. He could write the Psalms out of the overflow of his heart. One such psalm is a striking example of blessing and praising God for His mercy and forgetful forgiveness:

> Praise the Lord, O my soul;
> all my inmost being, praise his holy name.
> Praise the Lord, O my soul,
> and forget not all his benefits.
> He forgives all my sins
> and heals all my diseases;
> He redeems my life from the pit
> and crowns me with love and compassion.
> He satisfies my desires with good things,
> so that my youth is renewed like the eagle's.
> The Lord works righteousness
> and justice for all the oppressed.
> He made known his ways to Moses,
> his deeds to the people of Israel:
> The Lord is compassionate and gracious,
> slow to anger, abounding in love.
> He will not always accuse,
> nor will he harbor his anger forever;

He does not treat us as our sins deserve
   or repay us according to our inequities.
For as high as the heavens are above the earth,
   so great is his love for those who fear him;
as far as the east is from the west,
   so far has he removed our transgressions from us.
As a father has compassion on his children,
   so the Lord has compassion on those who fear him...
But from everlasting to everlasting
   the Lord's love is with those who fear him,
   and his righteousness with their children's children—
with those who keep his covenant
   and remember to obey his precepts.
                                   —Psalm 103:1-13,17,18

Parents, look at your dispositions. Proverbs 25:24 says that it is better to live in a corner of an attic than in a beautiful home with a cranky, quarrelsome woman. Fathers can be just as cranky, quarrelsome, and difficult to live with, so they are not exempt from self-analysis. We may have fostered this angry, sullen, resentful attitude in our teenagers unknowingly. You might ask your teenager how he honestly feels about the quality of your family life. Tell him that you're open to suggestions for change, that life is a two-way street requiring give-and-take from everyone. Be ready and willing to hear his complaints as well as his desires. *Communication* is the name of the game and is absolutely essential if authority is to be reestablished and right relationships nurtured.

Dr. Howard Hendricks, much-respected theologian and renowned lecturer on the home, is known for saying, "Heaven help the home!" He tells women they must be the magnet in the home, drawing husbands and children home at the close of each day with a warm magnetism that is irresistible. This provides necessary stability and an incentive for each family member to *want* to get home at the end of a busy day. His wife, Jeanne, a talented writer and speaker, speaks of the home and established traditions as being a kind of cohesive glue holding family members together and helping provide security in a fragmented world (see *Footprints,* by Howard and Jeanne Hendricks).

Dr. Hendricks voices what many parents feel after their last child has flown the coop and is on his own: "I have often wished that God could give us one set of practice children, then the second set for keeps. Perhaps our hang-up is in thinking we could ever do it right, even if we had 100 chances. Part of being human is our severe limitations, especially in light of the Fall's blast. Finiteness involves failure. There are no perfect parents. Ultimately the test is not only what we do but what our children do with what we have done—failures and all. We must open the door for them to try."[1]

Mary Crowley, president of Home Interiors and Gifts, Inc., a very successful businesswoman and a warm, loving Christian, says that love has a locale here on earth, and it is called *the home*. "Home is where love is nourished, where it is best expressed. Out of the home all other relationships are influenced. The home is the place where character is formed....The home should be a haven—a place of refuge, peace, harmony, and beauty....Many things in life tend to tarnish and must be polished frequently in order to stay new and shiny. Love, too, needs to be constantly shined and polished, protected, and nourished, lest it grow dim and lose its lustre."[2]

One of the things love does is to accept another person, warts and all. That is, we don't expect perfection and we don't necessarily have to approve of what someone does in order to accept him. Alienation with our adolescents often comes at that point. Because something he persists in saying or doing irritates us, we shut off our communication lines and he feels he is no longer loved and accepted.

No, we don't approve of some of their lifestyles. What parent likes to see her beautiful daughter move out and go to live with a man older than she? Who among us could sanction a lifestyle like that? Professional counselors tell parents caught in such heartbreak that they must accept their daughters and/or sons as they are. "We love you, but we don't approve of the way you are living." That leaves the door open. Even though the child has broken every rule you have established, still you are holding out unconditional love. Do we have a Biblical precedent for that? Indeed we do, in our Lord Himself. Jesus left the perfect example in His dealings with people. He didn't hand them a list of prescribed rules that would qualify them to experience His healing touch and His love. But in response to His unconditional love, *they* changed their behavior.

Relationships can be restored. Edith Schaeffer of L'Abri, lecturer and author of many fine books, says in speaking of the family, "We are endeavoring to preserve an endangered species—the family!" It may take a long time, even years, for right relationships to be restored, but I believe the effort is required of us as parents.

Let Go

In dealing with rebellion and kids who have gone against all parental authority, I counsel parents to look at the Biblical narrative of the prodigal son and his relationship with his father. The account can be found in Luke 15:11-32. The youngest son in the family asked for his share of the family estate, and not long after that he took off for a distant country and there squandered his wealth on wild living. You may be tempted to call the father foolish, but I assure you that he knew what he was doing.

The first thing to note about this father is that he let his son go. This is the hardest thing for a loving parent to do. When the child is leaving to go to college or into some profession and is a very responsible person, it's even hard then. But when a child is involved in wrong living and is ruining his life, just throwing it away and breaking your heart, you want to hold on, to cry out, to plead with him not to do it. You don't want to let him go. But please learn something from reading this Biblical narrative: you can't make him stay.

Parents have come to me saying, "Have you heard about the Jones kid? He ripped off his dad and mom and he split. Boy! If that was my kid, I'd have beat the tar out of him!"

I've been known to say to parents who talk like that, "Well, what would you do after you beat the tar out of him, and he got up, wiped his eyes dry, and still walked off?" The point is that there's no way you can make a kid stay home if he is intent on going his own way. Yes, he'll waste money, he'll live in squalor, he'll hurt himself and he'll go hungry. His shoes and his clothes will wear out, and he'll look exactly like some of those hitchhiking kids out there on the highway.

But remember, you don't own him.

God gives our children to us, but there does come a time when, if they choose to run away or live with someone of whom you disapprove—or whatever their choice is that goes against your wishes—you've got to let them go.

Dotson Rader, himself a runaway at one time, has crisscrossed the country researching the plight of the more than a million runaways yearly in the United States. Their average age is 15. About 35 percent of runaways leave home because of incest and 53 percent because of physical neglect. The rest are what Rader calls "throwaways"—children kicked out or simply abandoned by their parents.

But there are also kids who come from good families, who simply give up on the establishment and take off. More than 80 percent of runaways are from middle-class and upper-middle-class families. Rader says they seem starved for adult affection and regard but are fearful and filled with resentment against their parents whom they believe never loved them. These kids suffer from malnutrition, drug-related disorders, sexual dysfunction, and (having little access to medical care) disease. Runaways on the streets for more than a month usually end up as prostitutes because they have no other way to make a living. (These are both male and female prostitutes; a lot of the boys are victimized by homosexuals.)

When you read things like this, doesn't it make you all the more determined to work at the relationship with your son or daughter *before* it reaches the stage where your child takes off? If your boy or girl is younger than 13 then get in the car and chase after him or her all night. You can still exercise your authority and control when they are that young. But after they get on up into their teens, and if there is a history of rebellion, then, like the father of the prodigal, you won't have much choice. This father undoubtedly followed that boy with his prayers. He was a gracious father, not permissive, as some have implied in their writing. Dr. Norman Wright (marriage, family, and child counselor) explains that a permissive father would have given the son his money and let him go simply to get him out of his hair. And a permissive father wouldn't have staged a celebration upon the return of his son. Dr. Wright asks, "Why add a fatted calf to the rest of his losses?"

The Biblical narrative tells us that a famine came upon the land, and you can be sure a famine came upon the prodigal as well. We read that the son "began to be in need." Do you suppose he began to reflect upon what he had done? He had taken his money and run, but now he was coming to his senses. It's a familiar narrative that has been played out in the lives of countless young men and women who have turned their backs on their parents—but then comes the day of reckoning.

While the father was unmovable in his principles earlier, and was willing to be gracious in his ways instead of being hard, he was also patient. He demonstrated his rocklike qualities. He waited without giving up. And when his son made the decision to return home, while the boy was still a long way off his father saw him and was filled with compassion for him. "He ran to his son, threw his arms around him and kissed him" (Luke 15:20).

Patience Pays

The prodigal's father was patient enough not to demand an apology. The father didn't stand there with his hands on his hips and an angry look on his face, spitting out, "I told you! Look at the mess you've made of your life! Why didn't you listen to your mother and me? Get in here and apologize right now!" He didn't even tell the boy to take a shower and get cleaned up.

I want to suggest to you parents who have gone through this pigpen business with your adolescent, don't let the pig smell bother you when he returns. Demonstrate your love. Your love will bring out your child's own apology; this kind of patient loving will bring a demonstration of repentance through changed behavior. Here is your opportunity to practice loving and forgetful forgiveness.

This was a forgiving father. How do we know this? He ran to his son, hugged and kissed him, and threw a party for him! He showed his love by putting a ring on his finger and sandals on his fee, then ordering the servants to bring out the best robe. He said, "Let's have a feast and celebrate!'' The family ring was like a Visa or Master Card credit card today. He was giving the boy the family's line of credit. The past was over and put away; the irresponsibility of the son was no hindrance to fatherly faithfulness.

Whom do the father's actions remind you of? Most of us have ripped our heavenly Father off. We've stolen from Him and wasted the things He's blessed us with. Time after time we've come back and lisped, ''I'm sorry,'' and shortly thereafter we've gone on our merry way with not so much as a backward glance.

Try being like God to your children, and see what a difference it makes in your relationships. When we cut God off, does He cut us off? When the prodigal son cut off his relationship with his parents, did the father walk out on the son? Just remember, two severed lines of communication will make all further communication impossible! The challenge for us as parents is to be Godlike; this can happen as we grow and mature in Christ.

NOTES

1. Howard and Jeanne Hendricks, *Footprints* (Portland: Multnomah Press, 1981), pp. 85-86.
2. Mary C. Crowley, *Women Who Win* (Old Tappan, New Jersey: Fleming H. Revell, 1979), pp. 63-64.

11

Drawing Your Family Together Spiritually

The path of the righteous is like the first gleam of dawn, shining ever brighter till the full light of day.
Proverbs 4:18

Families that try to handle all their problems with the aid of community resources, schools, family counseling centers, therapists, psychologists, and their grandmother's philosophy will come up short in the end. We live in a society that believes man has the answer to all of man's problems. Many Christians, I am learning, are succumbing to that kind of thinking. Moms and dads feel empty, exhausted, trapped, and ready to throw in the towel. Is it any wonder that they look to outside sources for help?

This is not to say that the "helping professions" can't offer *some* help, but as one individual has observed, they are often so busy discovering new lifestyles that conflict with the purpose of the traditional family that they sometimes end up doing more harm than good. The traditional family is definitely under assault; our youth-oriented society, it frequently seems, has collaborated to bankrupt traditional family values. More than one parent has pinpointed a big part of the problem: self-centeredness. This Me-ism philosophy says that you don't have to fall in step with your parents' values—just develop your own. Our youth have been subjected to values clarification philosophy, in which all values are regarded as personal and relative. The ultimate criterion of choice is what feels right to each person. Guilt is thought to be imposed by restrictive religious indoctrination, and the child must be freed from such guilt and the moralizing of parents, ministers, teachers, or anyone.

Our children have been raised in an era that encourages immediate gratification. This has been fostered by the media and some very erroneous teaching concepts that have crept into many schools. This is not to imply that *all* education is disrupting the family, but to acknowledge that some powerful forces have been chipping away at basic parental rights. Jeane Westin (*The Coming Parent Revolution*) found that 78 percent of the parents she surveyed felt that forces outside the home have usurped much of their authority, either directly or indirectly. She shows how parents ranked a list of the four primary forces of disorganization they feel are pitted against them. First was *media/advertising,* which outdistanced its nearest rival, *education,* by nearly three to one. *Psychology* came third and *government* fourth, both with nearly identical percentages. The category *other* was included to discover additional negative forces as perceived by these parents. A significant number of parents rated their children's peers as powerful enemies of the family and usurpers of their authority.[1]

Commenting on this, Westin writes: "If parents are going to change the future, to be able to get up in the morning with the belief that they can make a better life for their families, they will have to find ways to regain control of child-rearing."[2]

Parents have always been the means of social change. This is historical fact with roots that can be traced to Biblical precedents. I am in agreement with Jeane Westin, who has stated it so well: "What we need is the family-centered family that turns inward to its values for strength."[3] This means a return to take-charge parenting—parents who refuse to be the scapegoats for a society who blames everything on them. And for Christian parents it means an all-out effort to draw your family together spiritually.

Getting Our Derailed Families Back on Track

The missing ingredient in most families is spiritual life. By rejecting God, the family has no *lasting* help outside its own limited resources. No community resource center or professional help can provide the stability and hope that comes through consciously acknowledging and relying on the Lord.

The Apostle Paul must have encountered some of the same types of problems which the family unit is experiencing today. In his Ephesian letter he makes a strong plea for unity in the body of Christ so that we may all be built up in the knowledge of the Son of God and become mature, attaining to the whole measure of the fullness of Christ (see Ephesians 4:13). Paul uses an analogy that relates to family life, and says, "Then we will no longer be infants, tossed back and forth by the waves, and blown here and there by every wind of teaching and by the cunning and craftiness of men in their deceitful scheming. Instead, speaking the truth in love, we will in all things grow up into him who is the Head, that is, Christ. From him the whole body, joined and held together by every supporting ligament, grows and builds itself up in love, as each part does its work" (Ephesians 4:14,15).

If we are to live as children of light, Paul explained to his Ephesian friends, there are certain things that we must do. He speaks of the futility of thinking as the world outside of Christ thinks, in which minds are darkened in their understanding and separated from the life of God because of the ignorance that is in them due to the hardness of their hearts. They lose their sensitivity and give themselves over to sensuality and indulging themselves in whatever they lust for (verses 17-19). Doesn't that sound familiar?

The first thing that must be done if we are to get our derailed families back on track is to help them get their minds straightened out. They've been corrupted by exposure to outside influences that are doing battle with the traditional family (see Ephesians 4:22), so they must "be made new in the attitude of their minds," and they must be shown and encouraged to developed a new self, "created to be like God in true righteousness and holiness" (verse 24).

Holiness has to do with separating ourselves from sin and becoming alive to God (see Hebrews 12:14). When children are young, they are very receptive and responsive to spiritual things, but as they become older (if they have not been nurtured this way) the job of drawing them into spiritual awareness becomes more difficult. I would urge you to draw upon the resources of your heavenly Father, who loves your children more than you do. He can be counted on to help you in this all-important responsibility.

Paul outlines some areas that we must work on. First of all, our children must be taught that no longer will lying be tolerated. No more trying to "pull the wool" over parents' eyes. A new and truthful openness with each other is required (Ephesians 4:25).

Anger must be dealt with—learning to control one's temper. And there must be no more stealing—not just outright thefts, but also the subtle stealing in which our kids expect a handout all the time, and don't want to be responsible around the house. Paul says we must all work, doing something useful with our hands (Ephesians 4:25-28).

Our conversation needs to be cleaned up. "Do not let any unwholesome talk come out of your mouths, but only what is helpful for building others up according to their needs, that it may benefit those who listen" (verse 29). This is a big area. Judging from the way I hear students speak on school campuses, I would say that parents have a big responsibility on their hands in this area. Foul language—dirty talk and gutter words—is all too common. But it's not just this problem, but also the disrespectful way that many adolescents talk back to their parents, along with their inconsiderate demands.

All of this grieves the Holy Spirit, the apostle warns, so "Get rid of all bitterness, rage and anger, brawling and slander, along with every form of malice. Be kind and compassionate to one another, forgiving each other, just as in Christ God forgave you" (Ephesians 4:31,32). In chapter 5 of Ephesians Paul continues his exhortation on living in unity and as children of light. "Live as children of light," he again urges, and this is accomplished by living a life of love, with Christ as our example. He again states that immoral living is improper for God's holy people. Then he strikes a new note—thanksgiving. We've got a generation of young people on our hands who think the world (and this begins with their parents) owes them everything. They think they have a right to take what parents so freely give without giving anything in return. Then, when they do have to go out into the world, they don't know how to function. Even a simple "Thank you" is missing from much of their conversation. It's as though it would be a sign of weakness (or somehow demeaning) to show gratitude!

One father explained it this way: "My kids were free boarders and rather unpleasant ones at that. They treated their home like a hotel and their mother and me like servants who should always be ready to drop everything and wait on them.

"I was too easy on them, thinking they'd only be kids once. Now it looks like they'll be kids all their lives."[4]

Another father woke up one day to what his kids had been doing and admitted, "I've been playing God in their lives—Daddy-God who gives handouts and who is always available for an extra ten bucks or whatever. When my son got married he didn't know how to handle money or responsibility. His poor little wife...." It works the same way with spoiled girls who get married and expect their young husbands to be just as available with handouts as Dad and Mom always were, and when the handouts aren't there they come trotting back to the folks.

How do we change this alarming direction? Take-charge parenting means that we establish a new reality, helping our children understand that there is a difference between what they want and what they need. If they want something, then they pitch in and work, making some kind of family arrangement to earn the extra money. A lot more could be said on this, but you get the idea: no more pampering, but teach responsibility and develop thankful hearts in your children.

Paul's final words in Ephesians 6 convey the idea that living as children of light in a darkened world means engaging in battle. Warriors must be equipped. More than one writer these days is likening the preservation of the family to doing battle. Dr. Tim LaHaye's books, in particular, have used that analogy. Earlier I quoted from Jill Broscoe's book *Fight for the Family*. The Christian family is under incredible attack, and God's people have begun to be part of the problem rather than part of the solution. Many Christian homes are just heaps of rubble, and it has never been more true that the hope for the Christian family is the mobilization of each of its members. We must join together in this battle to preserve our Christian faith, for if we do not we stand to lose a generation of young people to the godless forces seeking to undermine our influence.

Equipping Our Families

The armor of God that will make each family member able to stand his ground is this:

The belt of truth
The breastplate of righteousness
Feet readied for peace
The shield of faith
The helmet of salvation
The sword of the Spirit, which is the Word of God.

To this description in Ephesians 6:10-17 Paul adds these words: "Pray in the Spirit on all occasions with all kinds of prayers and requests" (verse 18). He tells us to be alert and to keep on praying (verses 18,19).

Drawing your family together spiritually means that you must take the lead in family togetherness, including family devotions. My greatest single spiritual heritage is the consistent family devotions which my parents had with us. Even though my dad is a preacher, my most important learning did not come from him behind the pulpit but from him at the head of the dinner table leading us in family devotions. The Bible was the central book in our family, and it became the central force in my life. Until we get back to the Word of God as the driving force in our family relationships, we don't stand a chance.

I think I've heard every excuse there is as to why families don't have devotions together. "We just can't get the family together—everybody is so busy going in different directions." But there are times, usually daily, when family members eat together. That's why I believe mealtime is the best time for family devotions.

A friend relates how she and her brother and sister were raised on the Bible being read three times a day—at every meal by their widowed mother, who assumed the spiritual headship of that home. "Did we like it? No, not necessarily, although we did become accustomed to it and expected it in the same way we expected food on the table. In later life I could look back, and verses and whole passages from the Bible could be recalled from memory. It was one verse in particular, remembered in that way, which brought me to a recognition at age 19 that I needed to make a personal commitment of my life to Christ. Parental religious heritage was no substitute for that personal relationship." This friend went on to become a writer of Christian books.

Such family devotions won't just happen by themselves. It's going to take a commitment from you as dads and moms, and then an insistence that everyone in the family must attend and participate. This isn't regimentation; this is looking after the spiritual needs of your household. This is putting first things first. This is just as important as providing clothing, food, and other earthly necessities. This is claiming God's promises for the eternal welfare of your family as you diligently instruct them and feed them from His Word.

How do you begin? By starting it. (See Colossians 3:23,24.) In Colossians chapter 3 Paul sets up rules for holy living for the Christians at Colosse. He begins by telling them, "Set your hearts on things above, where Christ is seated at the right hand of God. Set your minds on things above, not on earthly things" (verses 1,2). That speaks of priorities. What is really important to you as parents? What is your first priority? Is it the eternal welfare of your family? Then teaching them spiritual truth is a prerequisite.

In this area of family devotions, be creative. Do different things in your devotional times together. "Let the word of Christ dwell in you richly as you teach and admonish one another with all wisdom, and as you sing psalms, hymns and spiritual songs with gratitude in your hearts to God. And whatever you do, whether in word or deed, do it all in the name of the Lord Jesus, giving thanks to God the Father through him" (verses 16,17).

Many excellent ideas can be gleaned from resource books and materials. Take a trip to your local Christian bookstore and you will be pleasantly surprised at what you will find. You might let your kids lead the devotions a time or two a week. I know one family who pantomimed Christ's parables to drive the principles home. Another family gave everyone the assignment of writing out the Beatitudes into "Be Attitudes" in their own words. Memorizing Scripture together is an excellent idea. Concentrate on a few verses or one passage per week. All kinds of things can be done to hold the interest of everyone, even if there is a considerable age span in your family.

Another thing I like to encourage families to do is to invite their pastor or youth pastor over for dinner once in a while. Make a big deal out of it. "It's a privilege to have our pastor and his wife for dinner, kids...." I was with a family who told me that when their kids were growing up they made it a practice to have some member of the church family over every three months. ''We wanted them to come to appreciate the spiritual leaders in our church,'' this father explained, and it was a very significant part of his children's growing-up process.

There is something else you can do—set a spiritual goal with your family for the year. For many teenagers Christianity is a dead bird. It's a bore, it's snore time. It's up to you as parents to challenge them spiritually. Many families read through the New or the Old Testament from a different translation each year. Then they take turns in having a discussion afterward, with one person in charge of preparing some questions and/or leading the discussion. Devotions like this will hold a family together.

How about the goal of winning other people to Christ? Maybe you'll begin by naming one person, but through your prayers and concern for this individual your list will enlarge. Someone will say, ''Well, Dad, how did it go in your conversation with Mr. 'You-know-who' today?'' Then Dad can share his experience for that day. The chances are that everyone in the family will have someone he wants to reach. Can't you see the exciting possibilities in this? This is spiritual warfare in which the whole family has teamed up to do battle together!

Have you ever tried keeping a prayer journal? Record the prayer requests of family members and other people who have asked for special prayer. Out comes the list at family devotion time, and someone reads the list or else it's passed around so everyone can look at it again. (Such lists can become long.) What joy there is when a petition gets crossed off! ''God's done it again! He's answered prayer!'' And the family rejoices together.

There would be a real change in homes across America if Christians started spending time together in family devotions and prayer.

It's time that we recognize the dangers confronting the inner spirits of our children daily. We must prepare them to do aggressive battle.

This may require some adjustments in our lifestyles, but that is a small price to pay. If we are too busy in other pursuits, then we are just plain too busy.

NOTES

1. Westin, *The Coming Parent Revolution,* pp. 39-40.
2. Ibid., p. 40.
3. Ibid., p. 42.
4. Ibid., p. 194.

12

How Do I Pull My Wayward Child Into the Family Circle?

He who walks with the wise grows wise,
but a companion of fools suffers harm.

Proverbs 13:20

Incredible hurts. I could never begin to fathom the incredible hurts some of you have experienced or may even now be experiencing. Some of you moms have wept yourself to sleep night after night for months. Some of you dads drive your car out into the night just to get away for a while to weep for a runaway son or daughter. One woman told me she would get into her car and drive until she came to an isolated place, and then just scream. I hear you tell me these things, but I can't place myself in your shoes and truly understand your incredible hurts.

Still, you ask me, "How do I pull my wayward child into the family circle?"

Admit That They Are Lost

Stop making amends for your wayward child. Admit that he is lost. I meet parents all the time who are on the defensive. They're desperate for help, yet they continue to make excuses for their son or daughter. "Will you pray for my son?" they ask. "He's having a problem. Oh, he loves Jesus—he's a fine Christian boy—but he just can't stop sleeping with *that girl*." You wouldn't say that's an okay situation, would you? Not for somebody else, but if it were *your* child, I wonder if you would come up to me and make excuses. Would you tell me your son is "a fine Christian boy," and by the way you said "that girl" intimates that it's all *her* fault and your son is really without blame?

I have to tell parents that as long as they persist in covering up and refusing to admit that their child is lost they won't be able to pull him back into the family circle.

That's hard. I want to assure you that it gives me no pleasure to have to talk to parents that way.

A girl came to see me at one of our meetings and gushed, "Oh, wow, I just love Jesus with all my heart, but I've got a little problem. I just love God and want to serve Him with all my heart, but sometimes I lie. I mean, sometimes I just stretch things a little. I pray about it and I witness to people, and I just love Jesus...."

As I listened to that I was thinking "Such gibberish! Who does she think she's fooling?" Finally I couldn't take any more of it, and I interrrupted: "Hey, wait a minute, let's get something straight. The Bible says in 1 John 1 that if we claim to have fellowship with God, yet walk in the darkness, we lie and do not live by the truth. If we claim to be without sin, we deceive ourselves and the truth is not in us. If we claim we have not sinned, we make Him out to be a liar, and His Word has no place in our lives" (see 1 John 1:6-10).

I let that soak in for a minute while she sat there in stunned silence. I didn't counsel her about how to handle her problem; I just gave her the Word of God. "Listen to me," I said, and I wasn't soft-spoken, mild, and easygoing: "Revelation 21:8 says that all liars are going to hell. You tell me you love Jesus and are a Christian. You're not a Christian if you lie and continue to sin." Then I talked to her about repentance and getting her heart really cleaned out before God. "First John 1 also tells us that if we walk in the light as He is in the light, we have fellowship with one another, and the blood of Jesus, God's Son, purifies us from every sin" (see verse 7).

We knelt together, and she wept and gave her heart to the Lord. She went home and told her parents what happened. They exploded! They marched down to see me and lit into me. "Calling our daughter a liar! How dare you! How could you tell her she's not going to heaven? What do you mean by striking fear into her heart like that?"

One of the greatest problems that parents have, I sincerely believe, is admitting that *their* kids are actually lost, that a child of *theirs* isn't actually headed for heaven. They don't want to admit that *their* son or daughter is a sinner. But once parents will admit that they're lost—call it what you will, but come to grips with the reality and finality of sin and a life apart from God—then I believe there is hope. Your whole prayer life will change when you see the desperateness of the plight of your lost child.

Intercessory Prayer Moves The Heart of God

I've seen it happen many times—brokenness and intercessory prayer moves the heart of God. The whole approach of parents changes. Things in the family start changing. Let me point out some verses to you that will help you understand what it means to really get down to business with God in this matter of saving your child. Each of these verses has to do with having a contrite heart:

> The eyes of the Lord are on the righteous,
>   and his ears are attentive to their cry....
> The righteous cry out, and the Lord hears them;
>   he delivers them from all their troubles.
> The Lord is close to the brokenhearted,
>   and saves those who are crushed in spirit.
> A righteous man may have many troubles,
>   but the Lord delivers him from them all....
> The Lord redeems his servants;
>   no one who takes refuge in him will be
>   condemned.
>
> Psalm 34:15,17,18,19,22

> The sacrifices of God are a broken spirit;
>   a broken and contrite heart,
>   O God, you will not despise.
>
> Psalm 51:17

> This is the one I esteem:
> he who is humble and contrite in spirit,
> and trembles at my word.
>
> Isaiah 66:2

The Whole Family Must Sacrifice

Everything in the hospital comes to a screeching halt when someone is dying. Lights flash, distress calls are sounded, and nurses, doctors, and orderlies come flying from every direction. Everyone is on *alert*. A life is hanging in the balance. Not a second can be lost.

That's the way it should be in our families when one of our number has forsaken the Lord and is on his way to an eternity without Christ. How can I say it any stronger? The whole family *must* sacrifice. You ask me, "Rich, how do we pull our wayward child into the family circle?" and I must tell you, "The whole family pulls together, and it won't be easy. You *must* sacrifice."

Other family members may even feel jilted. "Jamie gets all the attention in this family." No, that kind of whining and thinking has got to go. Jamie is different. Jamie is going to hell unless he comes to Christ. Do you want your brother or your sister in hell when the rest of the family is in heaven?

Earlier I wrote that when a child refuses to follow your standards, turns away from Jesus, and expects you to just sort of look the other way, make excuses for him, continue to give him handouts, and pamper and indulge his every whim, you should be like a rock, unmovable, and you shouldn't compromise your principles. But you must also redouble your expressions of love. You must affirm your undying love for that child—and each family member must join in doing that—but you must not smile at sin. Remember the story of the prodigal son and his older brother's reaction (see Luke 15). With anger welling up, pouting and sullen, he struck out at his father *and* his brother: "Look! All these years I've been slaving for you and never disobeyed your orders. Yet you never gave me even a young goat so I could celebrate with my friends. But when this son of yours who has squandered your property with prostitutes comes home, you kill the fattened calf for him!" (See verses 29,30.)

The father of those two sons was very wise. I can imagine him holding out his arms to his eldest son and saying, "Look, dear son, you and I are very close, and everything I have is yours. But it is right to celebrate, for he is your brother; he was dead and has come back to life! He was lost and is found!'' (See verses 31,32 TLB.)

Perhaps he added words to this effect: "Son, things have been pretty depressed around here. Yes, your brother blew it and lost everything, but we have to practice forgiveness. Sin costs, but now your brother has come to his senses. Now is not the time for any of us to turn our backs on him.''

In your family, your children must recognize that it may look like you are condoning their sister's or brother's selfish lifestyle, but we can't ever stop loving someone just because they let us down. Love is a powerful force. The magnetism of family love focused on a wayward family member, coupled with the prayers of many people, can draw that alienated child back into the family circle.

Use Every Positive, Spiritual Force

You have been asking me, "How do I pull my wayward child into the family circle?" One of the most important steps you can take is to enlist the prayer support of Christian friends. Call your Christian friends and ask them to put your child on their prayer list. The Bible instructs us to "bear one another's burdens," and this often means that we must swallow our pride and not be afraid to open up to those who can support us in prayer. Turn every positive spiritual force in your child's direction. Remember, we are doing battle with a powerful enemy, and that child needs all the help he can get.

> Your enemy the devil prowls around like a roaring lion looking for someone to devour. Resist him, standing firm in the faith.
>
> 1 Peter 5:8,9a

The book of Hebrews speaks of Jesus' death as destroying him who holds the power of death—that is, the Devil (see Hebrews 2:14). First John 3:7-10 contrasts those who are children of God and those who are children of the Devil. These are important verses:

> Dear children, do not let anyone lead you astray. He who does what is right is righteous, just as he is righteous. He who does what is sinful is of the devil, because the devil has been sinning from the beginning. The reason the Son

of God appeared was to destroy the devil's work. No one who is born of God will continue to sin, because God's seed remains in him; he cannot go on sinning, because he has been born of God. This is how we know who the children of God are and who the children of the devil are: Anyone who does not do what is right is not a child of God; neither is anyone who does not love his brother.

In Ephesians 6:11 we are told to put on the full armor of God so that we can stand against the wiles of the Devil. James 4:7 instructs, "Submit yourselves, then, to God. Resist the devil and he will flee from you."

This calls for an all-out attack on the Devil, turning every positive, spiritual force in the direction of the wayward child. I like to encourage parents to enlist the help of their youth director at their church. Ask him to take your child out for lunch—even offer to pay for it—but get your child into the presence of those who can have an influence on him. Use every means at your disposal.

Start believing *and* living like your child is going to come back into the family circle and into a restored relationship with the Lord. When you confront your child, don't hesitate to say, "We're praying for you, others are praying for you, and we know things are going to change for you. We love you."

A young man walked into one of my services accompanied by his mother. After the service I was drawn to the two of them. I went over, put out my hand, and said, "What's your name, son?" His mother answered. I asked him if he had a job. His mother answered again. Finally I said, "What's the deal?" She said, "He hasn't spoken in several months. He's blown his mind on drugs. He can't relate." She asked me to have lunch with him.

When I picked him up there wasn't a "Hello" or anything. I don't know if you've ever talked to a wall for 45 minutes, but that would be comparable to what I experienced in talking to this young man. When we arrived at his home, I went in with him, laid my hands on his head, and prayed for him. "Jesus, give this boy's mind back to him, please. Let him recover his mind as the prodigal son came to his senses."

I told his mother I'd like to see the boy again in another week. One week later I was knocking on the door. The boy came to the door and I said, "Hi, how are you doing?" He said, "Fine." Astonished, I looked at him and said, "You spoke!" I shouted to his mother, "He just said 'Fine!' " Can you imagine her joy? Here was a mother who hadn't given up on her son, who had pointed every spiritual force in his direction, and who had prayed and believed for his healing and that he would come back to the Lord.

What happened was that God's Spirit broke through and awareness came back to this boy after I intensely prayed for the healing of his mind. When his mother realized that there was a change, she began reading the New Testament to him. She read it aloud four times in 48 hours with him lying on his bed. The first time he spoke to her he said, with tears streaming down his face, "Mom, will you read it again!" Psalm 107:20 tells us that God sent forth His Word and it healed them; He rescued them from the grave.

Visualize Your Family As a Small Church

First Peter 2:9 teaches that the home has direct access to God the Father. "But you are a chosen people, a royal priesthood, a holy nation, a people belonging to God, that you may declare the praises of him who called you out of darkness into his wonderful light."

We are to be as shining lights to everyone whose life is touched by ours. Our homes—our families—can be a powerful spiritual force in our communities. Our wayward children can be pulled back into the family circle as we concentrate all our energies on helping them to become a part of the greater kingdom of God on earth—the family of God. Jesus cautioned His disciples about worrying (see Matthew 6:25-34). After running through the list of things people commonly worry about, Jesus gave these thought-provoking words: "But seek first his kingdom and his righteousness, and all these things will be given to you as well" (verse 33). This is an unchanging principle that gets overlooked as we hurry our way through our parenting experiences. We are so busy and preoccupied trying to be good parents that our priorities get shifted around.

Parents, if I could spend time with each of you reading this book, I would hasten to remind you, even as Robyn and I have to remind each other, that husbands and wives need to spend time with Jesus, "seeking first His kingdom and His righteousness." And then we can be supportive of each other and our family, as well as the family of God—the church—as a powerful spiritual force equipped to do battle with the enemy of all our souls. The Apostle Peter said, "Trust yourself [and your children] to the God who made you, for he will never fail you" (1 Peter 4:19 TLB).

13

What the Bible Says About the Family

To understand more clearly God's model plan for parents and their children, my wife and I have searched the Bible for key verses to share with families who want to improve the quality of their family life.

Few people would dispute the fact that we are living in troublesome times. With the divorce rate soaring seemingly out of control at over 50 percent of all marriages, what is left are fractured relationships and the walking wounded. What is needed is something that will bind husbands and wives together so strongly that the tapestry of their lives cannot pull apart at the seams. That something is the Word of God. Then when the evil forces rip into our relationships, we are so firmly bound together that we cannot be separated.

A Special Relationship

Wherever we look in the Word of God, we come away impressed with the fact that parenthood is a God-given privilege, a high and holy calling, and a heavy responsibility. As we trace the beginning of families in the Old Testament, we see that God promised to bless not just individuals, but also a man's children and his children's children. Here are some verses.

> Know therefore that the Lord your God is God;
> he is the faithful God, keeping his covenant of

> love to a thousand generations of those who
> love him and keep his commands.
>
> Deuteronomy 7:9

> If you pay attention to these laws and are careful
> to follow them, then the Lord your God will
> keep his covenant of love with you, as he swore
> to your forefathers. He will love you and bless
> you and increase your numbers. He will bless
> the fruit of your womb.
>
> Deuteronomy 7:12,13a

The Whole Counsel of God

We must not fail to pass the truth on to our children that ''All Scripture is God-breathed and is useful for teaching, rebuking, correcting and training in righteousness, so that the man of God may be thoroughly equipped for every good work'' (2 Timothy 3:16,17).

> The plans of the Lord stand firm forever, the
> purposes of his heart through all generations.
>
> Psalm 33:11

God's Promise to Abraham and to Us

Abram was called by God and given a promise:

> I will make you into a great nation
>   and I will bless you;
> I will make your name great,
>   and you will be a blessing.
> I will bless those who bless you,
>   and whoever curses you I will curse;

and all peoples on earth
will be blessed through you.

Genesis 12:2,3

Thank God for His provision for families!

God also spoke to Jacob and made a promise to him:

I am God Almighty; be fruitful and increase in
number. A nation and a community of nations
will come from you, and kings will come from
your body.

Genesis 35:11

Kings came forth from the loins of Jacob, but so did common people. It doesn't matter what our vocation is; God is no respecter of persons. The Apostle Peter fully understood this and preached it with boldness:

I now realize how true it is that God does not
show favoritism but accepts men from every nation who fear him and do what is right.

Acts 10:34

God does not have favorites. We and our children are of infinite importance to Him. Parenthood is a high calling. We are given the opportunity to be procreators—creators on behalf of God Himself. Once we understand that, we cannot lightly view our holy calling as parents.

Called to Be Like God

But there is more to parenting than giving birth; we are called to be like God in our family and other relationships. This is a call for unconditional love. How did God love? The answer comes as we stand at the foot of the cross. If we remember this through all our parenting joys and woes, our responsibility as parents and our response will be colored differently:

> For God so loved the world that he gave his one and only Son, that whoever believes in him shall not perish but have eternal life.
>
> John 3:16

> Dear friends, let us love one another, for love comes from God. Everyone who loves has been born of God and knows God. Whoever does not love does not know God, because God is love.
>
> This is how God showed his love among us: He sent his one and only Son into the world that we might live through him. This is love: not that we loved God, but that he loved us and sent his Son as an atoning sacrifice for our sins.
>
> Dear friends, since God so loved us, we also ought to love one another. No one has ever seen God; but if we love each other, God lives in us and his love is made complete in us.
>
> 1 John 4:7-12

Now let us move on to consider additional verses which exemplify God's plan for parents and their children.

Jesus Our Example

First, let's look at the child Jesus:

> And the child grew and became strong; he was
> filled with wisdom, and the grace of God was
> upon him.
>
> Luke 2:40

Jesus Christ was God dwelling among us as man. He experienced firsthand each level of human development. As a child, Christ learned to accept His heavenly father's will for His life, but also He learned obedience to His earthly parents. And that's the way it must be for *our* children.

> Then he went down to Nazareth with them and
> was obedient to them.
>
> Luke 2:51

> And Jesus grew in wisdom and stature, and in
> favor with God and men.
>
> Luke 2:52

Later, as an adult, Jesus could say:

> I seek not to please myself but him who sent me.
>
> John 5:30

> For I have come down from heaven not to do
> my will but to do the will of him who sent me.
>
> John 6:38

The Greatest in the Kingdom of Heaven

A precious little child was used by Jesus, the Master Teacher, to teach us one of the most important lessons to be learned if we would be His followers. One of the things my wife and I are learning is that we can be taught by our son. Until the time we had our son we didn't fully understand what our parents meant when they said that *they* had learned a lot from us as their children. It may seem a paradox that parents can be taught by their offspring, but it was Jesus who showed us the truth in this. It happened when His disciples came to Him wanting to know who was really the greatest in the kingdom of heaven. Listen to Jesus' response, and watch what He did:

> He called a little child and had him stand among them. And he said: "I tell you the truth, unless you change and become like little children, you will never enter the kingdom of heaven. Therefore, whoever humbles himself like this child is the greatest in the kingdom of heaven. And whoever welcomes a little child like this in my name welcomes me.
>
> "But if anyone causes one of these little ones who believe in me to sin, it would be better for him to have a large millstone hung around

his neck and to be drowned in the depths of the sea. Woe to the world because of the things that cause people to sin! Such things must come, but woe to the man through whom they come!...

"See that you do not look down on one of these little ones. For I tell you that their angels in heaven always see the face of my Father in heaven."

Matthew 18:2-7,10

The Little Children and Jesus

Christ was very interested in families. He became indignant when the disciples tried to keep the children away from Him because they thought He should not be bothered by them. They quickly learned how wrong they were as Jesus lovingly extended His arms to the little ones:

Then little children were brought to Jesus for him to place his hands on them and pray for them. But the disciples rebuked those who brought them. Jesus said, "Let the little children come to me, and do not hinder them, for the kingdom of heaven belongs to such as these."

Matthew 19:13,14

The qualities that Jesus found so appealing in little children are qualities that should still characterize our lives as we grow and mature. These are timeless traits—lovableness, freedom from pretense and pride, teachableness, and trustfulness.

God Desires to Help Families

In the Gospels we see the compassionate Jesus. In particular is this true when He was dealing with the crowds who followed Him—those seeking miracles and those who wanted to learn from Him. In their expressions He saw hungry humanity and family faces. That same loving concern exists today.

> ...Jesus went to a town called Nain, and his disciples and a large crowd went along with him. As he approached the town gate, a dead person was being carried out—the only son of his mother, and she was a widow. And a large crowd from the town was with her. When the Lord saw her, his heart went out to her and he said, "Don't cry."
>
> Then he went up and touched the coffin, and those carrying it stood still. He said, "Young man, I say to you, get up!" The dead man sat up and began to talk, and Jesus gave him back to his mother.
>
> They were all filled with awe and praised God. "A great prophet has appeared among us," they said. "God has come to help his people."
>
> Luke 7:11-16

We must teach our children that this same love, expressed by Christ's physical presence while here upon earth, is available today through the power of His Holy Spirit. We are powerless families only insofar as we limit ourselves by refusing His outstretched love and help.

Submission: The Key

What causes fights and quarrels among you? Don't they come from your desires that battle within you?...You do not have, because you do not ask God. When you ask, you do not receive, because you ask with wrong motives, that you may spend what you get on your pleasures....Submit yourselves, then, to God. Resist the devil, and he will flee from you. Come near to God and he will come near to you. Wash your hands, you sinners, and purify your hearts, you double-minded....Humble yourselves before the Lord, and he will lift you up.

James 4:1-3,7,8-10

Submit to one another out of reverence for Christ.

Ephesians 5:21

Wives, submit to your husbands as to the Lord. For the husband is the head of the wife as Christ is the head of the church, his body, of which he is the Savior. Now as the church submits to Christ, so also wives should submit to their husbands in everything.

Husbands, love your wives, just as Christ loved the church and gave himself up for her to make her holy, cleansing her by the washing with water through the word, and to present her to himself as a radiant church, without stain

> or wrinkle or any other blemish, but holy and
> blameless. In this same way, husbands ought
> to love their wives as their own bodies. He who
> loves his wife loves himself. After all, no one
> ever hated his own body, but he feeds and cares
> for it, just as Christ does the church—for we
> are members of his body.... Each one of you
> also must love his wife as he loves himself, and
> the wife must respect her husband.
>
> Ephesians 5:22-30,33

These submission verses have come under a lot of fire in recent years
as even Christian women have been led astray by radical feminist voices.

But a careful reading of this passage clearly shows that when husbands
and wives really understand and accept what these verses say, there
should be no rebellion and trouble. This is not giving husbands license
to lord it over their wives in a demanding, repulsive way. The Apostle
Paul is calling for balance—a balance between the right attitude and
the desired action on the part of both husbands and wives.

When a husband loves his wife as Christ loved the church, it takes
a very hardhearted woman not to respond lovingly and willingly to
his requests. And when a wife accepts her husband's leadership and
obeys him lovingly so as to prompt him to treat her lovingly, these
problems have no occasion to arise.

Children and Parents

The Apostle Paul had some words for children within families also,
and for their parents as well:

> Children, obey your parents in the Lord, for this
> is right. "Honor your father and mother"—

which is the first commandment with a
promise—"that it may go well with you and
that you may enjoy long life on the earth."
Fathers, do not exasperate your children; instead, bring them up in the training and instruction of the Lord.

Ephesians 6:1-4

Along these same lines, in a letter to the Christians at Colosse, the
apostle wrote:

Fathers, do not embitter your children, or they
will become discouraged.

Colossians 3:21

Rudolf Dreikurs, a leading child psychiatrist, insists that "a misbe-
having child is a discouraged child." My wife and I have concluded
after many years of traveling and working with young people across
the country that what we often see in troubled teens is discouraged
kids. We are willing to give most parents the benefit of the doubt when
it comes to this because so many of them just aren't aware that they
aren't offering their kids enough encouragement. The Biblical model
of a truly effective Christian mom and dad shows parents who are
encouragers.

Fathers, don't scold your children so much that
they become discouraged and quit trying.

Colossians 3:21 TLB

I think we need to impress upon our children that our eyes are to be on the Lord. We need to tell them, "People will fail you—even parents." We also need to tell them what the Apostle Peter says in this regard: "Trust yourself to the God who made you, for he will never fail you" (1 Peter 4:19b TLB).

This brings us to a look into the Old Testament, where we find some powerful instructions on God's model plan for parents and their children.

Back to Basics

> Love the Lord your God with all your heart and with all your soul and with all your strength. These commandments that I give you today are to be upon your hearts. Impress them on your children. Talk about them when you sit at home and when you walk along the road, when you lie down and when you get up. Tie them as symbols on your hands and bind them on your foreheads. Write them on the doorframes of your houses and on your gates.
>
> Deuteronomy 6:5-9

Can you think of any time of the day that this doesn't cover? Isn't Moses telling the people that parenting is a 24-hour-a-day job? This is a never-ceasing job: sitting, walking, rising, and lying. Someone has suggested that in our modern idiom this is the equivalent of tying a string around our finger as a reminder not to forget our responsibility to our kids!

I think Moses was saying to saturate our home life with the truths of God's Word to the extent that loving the Lord with one's whole heart, soul, and strength is just as natural as breathing. Home should be so good to come to at the end of the day for our family that outside activities and other people, events, and things won't have the attraction and appeal that home does.

What Moses was saying was that parents need to prepare their children to face the world. The competition for loyalty is stiff out there. The adversary is real. It really goes without saying that Christian young people are prime targets. Let's look at the counsel of other Old Testament sages:

> Tell it to your children, and let your children
> tell it to their children, and their children to
> the next generation.
>
> Joel 1:3

> ...from everlasting to everlasting
> the Lord's love is with those who fear him,
> and his righteousness with their children's
> children—
> with those who keep his covenant
> and remember to obey his precepts.
>
> Psalm 103:17,18

> Unless the Lord builds the house,
> its builders labor in vain....
> Sons are a heritage from the Lord,
> children a reward from him.
> Like arrows in the hands of a warrior
> are sons born in one's youth.
> Blessed is the man

whose quiver is full of them.
They will not be put to shame
when they contend with their enemies in the
gate.

Psalm 127:1,3-5

Blessed are all who fear the Lord,
who walk in his ways.
You will eat the fruit of your labor;
blessings and prosperity will be yours.

Your wife will be like a fruitful vine
within your house;
your sons will be like olive shoots
around your table.
Thus is the man blessed
who fears the Lord.
May the Lord bless you from Zion
all the days of your life;
may you see the prosperity of Jerusalem,
and may you live to see your
children's children.

Psalm 128

One of the familiar and oft-quoted passages dealing with families is to be found in the book of Joshua. Joshua assembled all the tribes of Israel together and recited for them some of their history. He knew that death was close for himself, and so he reminded the people that "not one of all the good promises the Lord your God gave you has failed" (Joshua 23:14); then he also warned them of the Lord's judgment if they violated His covenant. Often the deathbed warnings of individuals have shaped the destiny of their families. Joshua is a case in point: these are words for families in every generation to ponder and heed:

> Now fear the Lord and serve him with all faithfulness...choose for yourselves this day whom you will serve...but as for me and my household, we will serve the Lord.
>
> Joshua 24:14,15

Exhortations from the Book of Proverbs

Actually the entire book of Proverbs needs to be read by families frequently. Its 31 chapters make the book easy to read at the rate of one chapter a day each month. By so doing we will insure that these practical truths are firmly fixed in our children's minds and engraved upon their hearts. Here are some of these Proverbs.

> Listen, my son, to your father's instruction
> and do not forsake your mother's teaching.
>
> Proverbs 1:8

> The Lord's curse is on the house of the wicked,
> but he blesses the home of the righteous.
>
> Proverbs 3:33

A wise son brings joy to his father,
but a foolish son grief to his mother.

Proverbs 10:1

He who brings trouble on his family will
inherit only the wind,
and the fool will be servant to the wise.
The fruit of the righteous is a tree of life,
and he who wins souls is wise....
Whoever loves discipline loves knowledge,
but he who hates correction is stupid.

Proverbs 11:29,30; 12:1

The wise in heart are called discerning,
and pleasant words promote instruction.

Proverbs 16:21

The righteous man leads a blameless life;
blessed are his children after him.

Proverbs 20:7

Train a child in the way he should go,
and when he is old he will not turn from it.

Proverbs 22:6

In Summary

My wife and I have been working with young people and their parents since 1972. We've prayed with them, played with them, and dealt with all kinds of their problems. We've dealt with kids who put gum under church pews; on the other end of the spectrum we've dealt with young people who have sacrificed their babies to the devil. In between these two extremes have been situations of every kind imaginable. But in every situation I can say that the Word of God ministers to *every* struggle and to *each* individual.

Robyn and I pray that this examination of God's Word as it relates to the family will challenge you to raise your expectations to a new level of what God wills to do for *your* situation.

Other Good
Harvest House Reading

PARENTS IN CONTROL
Bringing Out the Best in Your Children
by *David Rice*

Getting your children under control is not as difficult as it might seem. *Parents in Control* explores: 1) How do parents get out of control? and 2) How to bring out the best in your child. Written for every parent, whether single or married, *Parents in Control* combines insight with a "nuts and bolts" approach to solving family problems.

PARENTS TALK WITH YOUR CHILDREN
by *V. Gilbert Beers*

One of life's most intimate human relationships is that of parent and child. Nothing is more important for a parent than knowing how to reach the heart of his or her child. Nothing is more important for a child than having parents who share their hearts.

V. Gilbert Beers, father of five and bestselling author of *Little Talks About God and You* shares his experiences and insights and challenges parents to develop the kind of *talking relationship* with their children that will bring a lifelong friendship.

PARENTHOOD WITHOUT HASSLES—Well Almost
by *Kevin Leman*

You will find this book to be practical in every sense of the word. Its aim is to teach parents how to better understand themselves and their children and how to create situations in the home conducive to Christian growth and learning.

HOW TO DEVELOP YOUR CHILD'S TEMPERAMENT
by *Beverly LaHaye*

Clearly presents ideas and concepts on how you can more successfully develop and train your child as you gain insight into his or her temperament.

HANDLING YOUR HORMONES
by *Jim Burns*

Frank advice for today's youth on how not to compromise biblical convictions when faced with difficult issues such as parties, drugs and drinking, masturbation, venereal disease, and homosexuality.

Handling Your Hormones Growth Guide. A 64-page illustrated workbook with exercises and questions to help youth with their own views and feelings.

Handling Your Hormones Leader's Guide. Practical guidelines for creating an environment in which young people can deal openly and honestly with issues confronting them. For youth minister or lay leader.

STRESS IN THE FAMILY
How to Live Through It
by *Tim Timmons*

Inner and outer stress factors can destroy you and your family! Understanding the pressure you tolerate daily, you will discover *action-steps* that use stress to build you up rather than break you down.

THE FINAL CRY
by *Greg Laurie*

There is an epidemic sweeping our country today that is claiming the lives of young people at an alarming rate. It's the epidemic teenage suicide. Last year over 6,000 teenagers killed themselves and over 600,000 tried! Each day there is a suicide attempt at the rate of one per minute. Greg Laurie takes a powerful look at the reasons behind teen suicide and the hope and help that the church must offer to young people desperate for answers. A thirty-minute video is also available.

Another *Provocative* Book by
Bestselling Author
Rich Wilkerson

Rich Wilkerson tells us that "Few are exempt from some degree of private pain." Private pain may be emotional isolation, a sense of rejection, guilt, loneliness, depression, or other forms of inner anguish kept hidden from people. A powerful book that offers help and understanding and shows how suffering and pain need not devastate us but can be tools in the great Master Sculptor's plan for our lives.

Dear Reader:

We would appreciate hearing from you regarding this Harvest House nonfiction book. It will enable us to continue to give you the best in Christian publishing.

1. What most influenced you to purchase *Teenagers: Parental Guidance Suggested*?
   ☐ Author ☐ Recommendations
   ☐ Subject matter ☐ Cover/Title
   ☐ Backcover copy ☐ _____

2. Where did you purchase this book?
   ☐ Christian bookstore ☐ Grocery store
   ☐ General bookstore ☐ Other
   ☐ Department store

3. Your overall rating of this book:
   ☐ Excellent ☐ Very good ☐ Good ☐ Fair ☐ Poor

4. How likely would you be to purchase other books by this author?
   ☐ Very likely ☐ Not very likely
   ☐ Somewhat likely ☐ Not at all

5. What types of books most interest you?
   (check all that apply)
   ☐ Women's Books ☐ Fiction
   ☐ Marriage Books ☐ Biographies
   ☐ Current Issues ☐ Children's Books
   ☐ Self Help/Psychology ☐ Youth Books
   ☐ Bible Studies ☐ Other _____

6. Please check the box next to your age group.
   ☐ Under 18 ☐ 25-34 ☐ 45-54
   ☐ 18-24 ☐ 35-44 ☐ 55 and over

Mail to: Editorial Director
Harvest House Publishers
1075 Arrowsmith
Eugene, OR 97402

Name _____

Address _____

City _____ State _____ Zip _____

Thank you for helping us to help you in future publications!